Reshaping the Supreme Court

Anne B. Rierden

Reshaping the Supreme Court
New Justices, New Directions

Franklin Watts
New York/London/Toronto/Sydney/ 1988
An Impact Book

FOR STEVEN

Photographs courtesy of
UPI/Bettmann Newsphotos: pp. 16,
50, 63, 65, 81, 100, 115 (all);
The Bettmann Archive, Inc.: pp. 27, 30, 41.

Library of Congress Cataloging-in-Publication Data
Rierden, Anne B.
Reshaping the Supreme Court: new justices, new directions /
Anne B. Rierden.
p. cm.—(An Impact book)
Summary: Discusses the evolution of the Supreme Court's role and
its impact in politics and society, examines important decisions of
the Burger and Warren courts, and looks at new justices and issues
facing the present court.
Bibliography: p.
Includes index.
ISBN 0-531-10512-1
1. United States. Supreme Court—History—Juvenile literature.
2. Political questions and judicial power—United States—History—
Juvenile literature. [1. United States. Supreme Court.]
I. Title.
KF8742.Z9R53 1988
347.73'26'09—dc19   87-25958   CIP   AC
[347.3073509]

Contents

Reshaping the Supreme Court

The Supreme Court Today

1

On June 17, 1986, President Ronald Reagan walked into the White House briefing room to make a surprise announcement: the resignation of Chief Justice Warren E. Burger from the United States Supreme Court. In his place Reagan nominated Associate Justice William Rehnquist, the Supreme Court's most articulate conservative member. And to fill Rehnquist's seat, Reagan selected another ardent conservative, U.S. Appeals Court Judge Antonin Scalia. Reagan left the podium with a twinkle in his eye. Not only had he and his administration kept the announcement a secret for weeks, but he had also taken a giant step toward reshaping an institution that will reflect his views long after he leaves the White House.

The business of appointing Supreme Court justices is of enduring importance. Legal decisions made by these nine individuals can powerfully shape our lives. When two friends exchange secrets over the telephone without worry that others are listening, when blacks sit in the same classroom as whites, when workers join a union, they all enjoy rights that would not exist if the Supreme Court had not secured them for all Americans.

Presidents, by their power to appoint Supreme Court justices, can play a big role in charting the direction of the Court. The addition of a new justice can prompt a change in the Court's perspective. That is what happened during the mid-1930s to early 1940s when President Franklin Roosevelt had the chance to name eight new justices. His appointments shifted the Court from a conservative to a liberal position. In other words, it had generally supported government authority over an individual's claim. Now, with the influence of new justices, the Court was more willing to uphold the individual's claim.

Today with four Supreme Court justices over age seventy-eight, and two of those four in poor health, law scholars predict that President Reagan may be given a similar opportunity. Appointing Justice Scalia to the Court and elevating Rehnquist to chief justice, say Court observers, does not immediately signal a shift in its direction, but it will change the Court's chemistry and, invariably, its decisions. Both men are well known for their sharp intellectual vigor and appealing personalities, both of which are important factors in the making of decisions. Most experts agree, however, that if Reagan hopes to achieve a solid conservative majority on major social policy issues, he will most likely need to make additional appointments.

REAGAN'S AGENDA

When President Reagan first came to office, in 1981, he called for changes in several areas of social policy. Some of these proposed changes included the following:

- Amending the Constitution to ban abortion
- Restoring voluntary prayer in public schools
- Discarding the practice of quotas and ratios used in affirmative action programs designed to end racial injustice
- Ending the practice of required busing as a way to achieve racial balance in the schools

- Relaxing certain laws that protect persons accused of a crime
- Redirecting power from the federal government to state and local governments.

Unable to win Congress over to his views on these key issues, Reagan has targeted the federal courts as the vehicle to help carry out his policies. It is estimated that by the time Reagan ends his second term in office in 1988, he will have appointed half of the country's 743 federal judges. Of those appointments, two, Sandra Day O'Connor and Antonin Scalia, filled Supreme Court vacancies. Said one White House official after the nomination of Scalia, "It became obvious to us that the courts were the only recourse we have for the issues we care about. Now we have a chance of prevailing."

For the most part, the Supreme Court under Warren Burger did not respond to the Reagan administration's conservative agenda. The Burger Court failed to reverse its 1973 landmark abortion ruling, *Roe* v. *Wade*. It barred prayer in public schools and ignored the administration's insistence that affirmative action remedies be limited only to persons who could prove they'd suffered past discrimination.

Eager to appoint justices who might help carry out his administration's policies, Reagan has long prepared for any possible resignations. According to a June 1986 *Time* magazine article, the Justice Department had compiled a list of potential Supreme Court nominees at the beginning of Reagan's first term in office. The list included three U.S. Court of Appeals judges, Robert Bork, Scalia, and Richard Posner—all aggressive conservatives who would likely challenge many liberal Supreme Court rulings. Eventually, the list was narrowed to Scalia and Bork, and in the end Scalia won out as the more appealing candidate. First, Bork was ten years older than Scalia, who was just fifty and could remain on the Court past the year 2010. Second, Scalia would be the first Italian-American appointed to the Court, which from the administration's standpoint, seemed a good political move. Finally, the administration believed that Scalia's outgoing personality might help him build a conservative alliance on the Court.

Such an alliance was lacking in the Burger Court. Burger himself was criticized often for his inability to form strong majorities among the court's conservative members. This, observers say, resulted in a Court that lacked unity, leadership, and direction. And a Court that overruled few of the Warren Court's (1953–1969) decisions.

THE WARREN LEGACY

Noted for its liberalism, the Warren Court's rulings profoundly changed American law. Experts say that the Court's ability to make such monumental strides was due in part to its chief justice. Earl Warren was a master coalition builder. As a result, his strong liberal majority interpreted the Constitution to order such far-reaching changes in the law as the desegregation of public schools and the expansion of criminal rights. But to some, this "activism" was perceived as an abuse of judicial power.

Among the Warren Court's most severe critics was President Richard Nixon, who set out to topple the Court's landmark decisions by appointing conservative justices who believed the Constitution should be interpreted strictly. Among the decisions Nixon hoped his justices would overturn was the controversial *Miranda* v. *Arizona*.

The ruling ordered police to inform criminal suspects of their rights upon arrest. To Nixon, *Miranda* and other decisions upholding the rights of criminal suspects, only served to hinder police in enforcing the law. He promised the American people that his Supreme Court justices would shift the Court away from its liberal path and guide it toward a more conservative direction.

So far, the conservative counterrevolution sought by Nixon has not occurred. In a 1982 study on its record: "The Counter-Revolution That Wasn't," *New York Times* columnist Anthony Lewis wrote, "It is fair to say, in fact, that the reach of earlier decisions on racial equality and the First Amendment has been enlarged. Even the most hotly debated criminal issue, Miranda, stands essentially unmodified."

Instead, the Burger Court secured the Warren Court's liberal ideals by taking a middle-of-the-road course. The Burger Court did adopt a narrower view of some of its predecessor's rulings, but for the most part, the Warren legacy remains intact.

JUDICIAL ACTIVISM
VERSUS
JUDICIAL RESTRAINT

Like Nixon, Reagan would like to see many of the Warren Court's rulings cut back. He too has promised to appoint conservative Supreme Court justices. Speaking to a group of United States district attorneys in October 1985, Reagan said, "The independence of the Court from improper political influence is a sacred principle. The Founding Fathers knew that, like any other part of government, the power of the judiciary could be abused. They never intended, for example, that the Courts" try to replace legislative goals or compel "the populace into adopting anyone's views of utopia." He added that he would appoint to the bench lawyers who practiced "judicial restraint," and who would not view the courts "as vehicles for political action and social experimentation."

Supporters of judicial restraint believe that the Court should refrain from deciding social policy and also limit its interference with other branches of government. On today's Court, conservative Justices Rehnquist and O'Connor are considered the Court's strongest supporters of judicial restraint. Scalia's past record as an appeals court judge indicates he will follow the same course.

The opposite view and the one most opposed by the Reagan administration is "judicial activism." A court's activism generally means its willingness to make changes in public policy, particularly those established by other institutions. The most visible signs of judicial activism are decisions that overturn laws passed by Congress or executive policies. The Warren Court's decisions ordering states to desegregate their public schools stands as the most noted example of judicial activism. On today's Court, liberal justices Thurgood Marshall and William Brennan believe an activist Court is necessary to protect individual rights that may be ignored by the states, such as the right to remain secure in our homes.

One of the most visible and outspoken opponents of judicial activism is United States Attorney General Edwin Meese. He has bitterly accused the Supreme Court of exercising too much power. Referring to the Court's rulings over the past forty years, Meese believes it has strayed from the "original intentions" of the men who wrote the Constitution in 1787. For example, Meese and other Reagan administration officials believe the Warren Court took too much liberty in creating a constitutional right to privacy. Here the Court proclaimed that the Constitution "implicitly" guarantees all Americans the right to make individual choices such as those concerning marriage, sex, and the family without government interference.

Critics of the administration's view, such as Justice Brennan and law scholar Arthur Selwyn Miller, contend that it is impossible to always determine what the Constitution's drafters had in mind. First of all, they argue, the Constitution's language is not always clear. Ever since the framers wrote the document two hundred years ago, courts have struggled with the true meaning of such phrases as "due process" and "equal protection." This alone makes it difficult to understand the document's original intention.

Also, unlike the current administration, Brennan and others believe that the Constitution's intention is to adapt to society's changing needs. Justices, they say, should interpret the document from that perspective.

The arguments over judicial restraint or activism and over the Constitution's "original intention" are likely to recur as the Court considers cases involving state and federal power, abortion, affirmative action, the separation of church and state, capital punishment, and other criminal law matters. Which view the Court will adopt depends largely upon the number of justices Reagan can appoint.

Even if Reagan has the opportunity to appoint more justices, chances are he will not be pleased with every decision they make. History offers several examples of disappointed presidents. When Theodore Roosevelt's appointee, Oliver Wendell Holmes, Jr., refused to uphold a piece of antitrust legislation, the disgruntled president exclaimed, "I could carve out of a banana a judge with more character than that!"

Chief Justice Earl Warren and Associate Justice Brennan—both Eisenhower appointees—horrified the president with their rulings on criminal law and civil rights. More recently, Reagan appointee Sandra Day O'Connor has gone against the administration on some major issues, including school prayer and affirmative action. Experts agree, however, that in choosing Rehnquist and Scalia, both strongly committed to conservative ideals, Reagan may have limited those risks.

REAGAN'S APPOINTMENTS

Since his appointment to the Court in 1971, Rehnquist has provided the Court's most consistent vote for limiting the

In a surprise news briefing on June 7, 1986, President Reagan announced the retirement of Chief Justice Warren Burger (far right). At the same time, the president took a major step toward reshaping the Court by appointing Associate Justice William Rehnquist (second from right) to the position of Chief Justice and Antonin Scalia (left) to Associate Justice.

rights of criminal suspects. In 1984 he wrote an opinion creating the first exception to the *Miranda* rule. The change permits the police to question suspects without prior warnings in the interest of "public safety."

He has dissented from most of the Court's decisions upholding various remedies for racial discrimination, from busing to affirmative action. Rehnquist was the only dissenter in the 1983 case that upheld the federal government's policy denying a federal tax deduction for Bob Jones University, which discriminates against blacks.

As for Scalia, he has openly criticized several major Supreme Court rulings and has supported positions that agree with the Reagan administration's conservative legal and political agenda. For example, although he has not ruled on an abortion case, he did state in 1978 that the courts "have no business" deciding such cases.

He has also sided with the administration by consistently expressing a narrow view of the First Amendment's freedom of speech guarantee. In one case, Scalia found no First Amendment rights for homeless demonstrators who slept across the street from the White House. Instead, he blasted their claims that they were exercising their freedom of speech by sleeping.

Although it is too early to assess any of Scalia's Supreme Court opinions, conservatives and liberals alike have no doubt that he will help fortify the Court's conservative wing.

THE COURT'S LINEUP

Six presidents have had a hand in appointing the current nine justices of the Supreme Court, each of whom holds a lifetime term. The philosophical alliances of today's Court are splintered into three categories: liberals, conservatives, and moderates. Below is a short summary of how each justice generally votes.

On the left, Justices William Brennan and Thurgood Marshall form the Court's liberal bloc. Though these liberals are among the Court's oldest members, they are not likely to retire soon. Both know that many of the liberal doctrines they have fought for could be abandoned if Reagan appoints their replacements.

On the right can be found Rehnquist and Sandra Day O'Connor (the Supreme Court's first female justice and Reagan's first appointee), and now Scalia. The three conservatives are the Court's youngest members and more than likely will serve into the next century.

In the middle the moderates, Justices Harry Blackmun, John Paul Stevens and Byron White provide the "swing vote," out of which majorities are formed. For example, if four justices feel strongly about one side of an issue and four others are clearly on the other side, the justice whose views are not known becomes the swing vote. Until his retirement in June 1987, Justice Lewis Powell also fit into the moderate category.

As stated earlier, it is not always easy to gauge how a justice will vote in every case. Labeling a justice as a conservative, moderate, or liberal is generally sufficient, yet justices can and do switch alliances. So-called conservatives have been known to vote liberal and vice versa. Justice Harry Blackmun was considered conservative when he first joined the Court in 1970. Two years later he wrote the opinion in one of the Court's most liberal decisions, giving a woman the right to have an abortion.

The Court will likely change O'Connor and Scalia as it has changed Blackmun and every outstanding justice throughout its history. As for Rehnquist, who was first appointed to the Court in 1971, it appears that he is in the process of change. In a 1985 *New York Times* article, Rehnquist said he at first presumed his task on the Court was to reverse the liberal trend of the Warren Court, "to kind of lean the other way." Now he says, "I think I see it quite differently. . . . There probably are things to be seen on both sides of the issue that I perhaps didn't always think were there."

THE ISSUES

How Chief Justice Rehnquist and the associate justices decide today's major issues will have a great impact on American society. The following legal issues remain closest to the hearts of the American public.

Abortion: This controversial topic reached the Supreme Court as a constitutional question in 1972. In *Roe* v. *Wade* and *Doe* v. *Bolton* the Court set limits on state power to prohibit or regulate abortion. In its ruling, the Court invalidated statutes in Texas and Georgia prohibiting abortion and with them statutes from many other states.

Basing its decision upon when the fetus can survive outside the mother's womb, the Court ruled that states can regulate abortion only after the third month of pregnancy. After the sixth month, at which the fetus becomes viable (able to survive outside the mother's womb), the state may prohibit abortion unless the mother's life is endangered. Today's Court stands narrowly divided on the abortion issue, with only five liberal votes upholding the *Roe* ruling. Experts say that the Court's conservative justices would probably not ban abortion but rather ask the states to decide the issue, as was the case before 1973.

Affirmative Action: Affirmative action concerns efforts by colleges, government agencies, and companies doing business with the federal government to design hiring and college admissions programs to help women and minorities compete. Those who support these "affirmative action" programs believe they should remain in effect until racial minorities have caught up to the educational and employment levels of whites. Those opposed to the programs believe that race or gender should not be taken into account when considering applicants for jobs or college admissions. According to this view, affirmative action is a form of "reverse discrimination" against white males.

The case *Regents of the University of California* v. *Bakke* (1978) brought the debate to a head. Here, in a complex opinion, the Supreme Court established that colleges could consider race in applications but that quotas were unconstitutional. The Reagan administration argues against affirmative action, believing that the uses of racial preference in job hiring or promotional practices discriminates and is therefore unconstitutional. Since the Court has remained splintered on this issue, it is difficult to predict its future. Reagan will need other appointments to make his views triumph.

Criminal Law: The number one focus in this area is the exclusionary rule. The rule prescribes that any evidence confiscated by illegal means—including confessions obtained before reading a suspect's rights, unauthorized wiretapping, or the seizing without a warrant of tangible evidence like drugs—cannot be used in a criminal trial. The debate on this issue is between those who support an expansion of the rights of persons accused of crimes and those who advocate the right of society to protect itself. In the past, convicted persons have been set free or given new trials where illegal evidence has been introduced, but the Burger Court modified these rulings by favoring police and prosecutors' claims over suspects' rights. Reagan would like to see past rulings upholding the exclusionary law overturned, and the Court's conservative members appear determined to make that happen.

Separation of Church and State: For decades the Court has had to walk the line between two clauses of the First Amendment: the "establishment" and "free exercise" clauses. The establishment clause forbids Congress from passing any law making any religion the religion of the United States. It also creates a "wall of separation" between church and state. Rulings where the Court has banned prayer and Bible readings in public schools and prohibited religious symbols in public places fall under the establishment clause category.

The free exercise clause says that the government cannot take away the freedom to worship as one pleases. It became the issue in 1940 when a Jehovah's Witness, who viewed flag saluting as idolatrous, charged that public schools, in forcing his children to pledge allegiance to the flag, denied them freedom of religion. The Court ruled against him in *Minersville School District* v. *Gobitis*, stating that the flag salute "awakened" in the child's mind "a sense of national unity," and was therefore important. The Gobitis children would either have to salute the flag or attend a private school.

The Burger Court has expanded the separation of church and state in some areas, yet lessened it in others. It allowed parents of parochial school children to receive federal tuition tax credits, but struck down "moments of silence for prayer" in public schools. The conservative members of today's Court favor less separation and are willing to "accommodate" expressions of religious belief such as nativity scene displays in public places. Liberal members believe in maintaining a strict wall of separation between church and state. The final chapter in this two hundred-year-old battle is far from over.

Freedom of the Press: In rulings on this First Amendment issue, the Court in 1964 established rules to broaden the freedom of newspapers and magazines to write and respond to public issues. In close decisions the Burger Court mostly favored the press. Conservative members, however, have indicated the need for stricter restraints on the press. Chief Justice Burger, for example, vehemently rejected requests that the Court's proceedings be open for broadcast. On the liberal side, Justice Brennan, who strongly favors a free press, considers it important that the proceedings be televised. "Ours is a public proceeding," he countered. "And there is no reason in my judgment why only those who can gain entrance to the courtroom should be able to witness those proceedings."

How the Supreme Court decides the legal questions in these issues will indeed affect the course of our lives as individuals, as communities, and as a nation. And the political views of Supreme Court justices will largely determine the Court's decisions. Since the future of many aspects of our lives, from the economy to the choices we make in our personal lives, rests in part on whom a president appoints to the Supreme Court, it is important that we try to understand this complex relationship. The purpose of this book is to examine that relationship against the backdrop of recent appointments to the Court and what those appointments may mean for its future direction.

The Court's Foundations

2

The Supreme Court of the United States was created by Article III of the Constitution, which states, in part, "The judicial power of the United States shall be vested in one Supreme Court, and in such inferior courts as the Congress from time to time shall ordain and establish." The Constitution, therefore, established the Supreme Court but left the details of the Court's exact organization up to Congress. Basically, the Court's role is to decide whether the actions of the president, Congress, the states, and lower courts are in accord with the Constitution, in order to ensure that the constitutional rights of Americans are not violated.

THE CONSTITUTIONAL CONVENTION

Before the signing of the Constitution on September 17, 1787, the Articles of Confederation governed the United States. Under this document, the majority of government business was settled in a one-house legislature called a Congress. There was no separation of legislative and executive branches and no national court system.

The absence of a federal judiciary was considered a major drawback in the Articles. Political statesmen Alexander

Hamilton and James Madison stressed the need for a strong national court system that could try persons accused of committing crimes against the Union and settle disputes between the states. At the time, any national legal disputes had to be settled through the poorly constructed and highly imbalanced state government systems.

In May 1787, Madison and other leading statesmen brought together fifty-five state delegates to meet in Philadelphia and draw up a plan to create a stronger government and more orderly society. Every delegate who participated in the Constitutional Convention, as it was called, agreed that a national judiciary should be established. They disagreed, however, on how that judiciary would be formed.

Those who favored a powerful national government proposed the Randolph Plan, designed to set up a Supreme Court and lower federal courts. Those who advocated strong and independent state governments countered with the Paterson Plan, calling for the establishment of one supreme federal court. Supporters of the Paterson Plan and states' rights believed additional federal courts would give the national government too much power over state governments in deciding judicial questions. With the Paterson Plan, state court could hear cases in the first instance, then, if needed, cases would go directly to the Supreme Court on appeal.

The conflict between the states' rights advocates and the nationalists was brought to a compromise in Article III of the Constitution. Since the Article left to Congress the question of whether to establish lower federal courts, the conflict was postponed until the new government went into operation.

CREATING A
FEDERAL JUDICIARY

Action on the federal judiciary came soon after the ratification of the Constitution. When the new Congress convened in 1789, finalizing the structure of the country's court system became the first order of business. In the first Senate debates, the question again arose over whether lower federal courts should be established at all or whether state courts should hear all federal claims. The controversy divided Congress.

Again states' rights supporters argued that state courts could preside over federal cases (for example, those cases involving an individual against the United States government, or those involving individuals from different states) and if unable to reach settlement on that level could go directly to the Supreme Court for review. With this system the federal government could not take away state powers. Those who favored a strong national government expressed suspicions that state courts would prejudice persons from other states by dealing with them unjustly. This latter group favored a lower federal court system.

After months of debate, Congress passed the Judiciary Act of 1789, setting up a federal judicial system composed of a Supreme Court, with a chief justice and five associate justices; three circuit courts comprising two Supreme Court justices and a district judge; and thirteen district courts, each presided over by a district judge. Through the Judiciary Act, Congress exercised immediately its power to establish lower courts.

WASHINGTON'S
APPOINTMENTS

The Constitution gave the president, upon the advice and consent of the Senate, the power to appoint federal judges and justices. The job of appointing the first Supreme Court justices went to George Washington, the only president ever to have had the opportunity to appoint the entire federal judiciary. In doing so, Washington established an important tradition. He appointed justices with whom he was politically compatible. The first Supreme Court justices, like their appointer, all subscribed to the Federalist Party credo: a belief in a strong national government.

Washington named as chief justice John Jay, an experienced judge, lawyer, and drafter of New York's first constitution. The remaining justices, James Wilson, John Rutledge, William Cushing, John Blair, and James Iredell, were all lawyers and competent statesmen. The Court met for the first time on February 1, 1790, in the Royal Exchange Building located in what is now New York's Wall Street district. In comparison to today's Court, the first session was unimpressive. Only four of the justices attended—Jay, Wilson, Cushing, and Blair, with the session lasting only ten days.

By the end of the Court's first decade, it had decided only about fifty cases. One of these decisions, *Chisholm* v. *Georgia*, embroiled the Court in considerable controversy. The case involved property held by the state of Georgia that two South Carolinians believed belonged to them. The Supreme Court agreed to hear the South Carolinians' suit against Georgia and thus for the first time allowed a citizen from one state to sue another state in federal court. When the Court ruled in favor of the South Carolinians, Georgia raged. States' rights forces assailed the ruling, saying it gave the federal court too much power over state concerns. By popular consent, Congress adopted the Eleventh Amendment, forbidding any federal court to try a lawsuit against a state by citizens of some other state. Thus, for the first time, the people overruled a Supreme Court decision.

Apart from this controversy, the Court held a quiet and unimportant place in federal government. As a result of its

John Jay, the first
Chief Justice of the
United States

uneventful workload, Chief Justice Jay and Justice Rutledge resigned from the Court early in their tenure to seek more challenging positions in state government. Rutledge became chief justice of South Carolina and Jay became governor of New York.

THE MARSHALL COURT

The position of the Court shifted dramatically with the appointment of John Marshall as chief justice in 1801. Considered by law historians as the country's greatest chief justice, Marshall dominated the Court to a degree unequaled by any other justice. He used his acute intellectual abilities and legal craftsmanship to carry forth policies that he favored, particularly those advancing the strength of the national government.

As his biographer Leonard Baker points out, the Supreme Court under Marshall operated "as an institution, and in doing so sought and achieved a moral force as great as that obtained by the presidency and Congress." The chief justice wrote 519 of the 1,106 opinions issued while he served on the Court. In addition, Marshall delivered thirty-six of the sixty-two decisions involving major constitutional questions. His opinions brought dignity to a fledgling Court and breathed life into the new Constitution.

In Marshall's most historic opinion, *Marbury* v. *Madison*, the Court established the doctrine of *judicial review*. The term refers to the Court's power to review acts of Congress, state laws, and executive orders in light of the Constitution. If the actions of these parties go beyond constitutional limits, the Court can declare them unconstitutional and, therefore, void. The idea was outlined in the persuasive commentary *The Federalist Papers*. Published after the Constitutional Convention by three of the Constitution's strongest advocates, Alexander Hamilton, James Madison, and John Jay, the series of essays urged the states to ratify the new document. In a section dedicated solely to the role of the federal courts, Hamilton describes the concept of judicial review.

It is the responsibility of the Court, he wrote, "to declare all acts contrary to the manifest tenor of the Constitution void." The Constitution is the supreme law and "no legislative act . . . contrary to the Constitution can be valid. To deny this would be to affirm that the deputy is greater than his principle; that the servant is above his master; that the representatives of the people are superior to the people themselves."

Hamilton explained that Congress could not serve as the judge over the constitutionality of its own acts. He argued that the courts must stand between the people and the legislature "to keep the latter within the limits assigned to their authority. The interpretation of the laws is the proper and peculiar province of the courts."

Marshall, too, had stated his position early on. Arguing for the adoption of the Constitution at the Virginia Ratifying Convention of 1788, he spelled out the doctrine of judicial review. "If Congress makes a law not warranted by any of the powers enumerated, it would be considered by the judges as an infringement of the Constitution which they are to guard. They would not consider such a law coming within their jurisdiction. They would declare it void."

Later, in his decision in the famous case *Marbury* v. *Madison*, Marshall cemented the doctrine of judicial review, proclaiming the supremacy of the Constitution over acts of Congress. The case actually began the night before Marshall began serving as Chief Justice. Prior to his appointment to the Court by President John Adams, Marshall had served as Adams's secretary of state. One of his duties was to fill out and deliver commissions for the office of justice of the peace, giving several individuals the power to perform marriages. By midnight, March 3, 1801, Adams's last night in office (he had been defeated for reelection by Thomas

Jefferson), Marshall had filled out and delivered all but a few commissions. The rest were left on the desk of James Madison, the incoming secretary of state under Jefferson. The next day, Jefferson ordered that any commissions left on Madison's desk not be delivered.

William Marbury's commission to serve as justice of the peace for the District of Columbia was one of those not delivered. Without it, he could not begin serving his term. Infuriated, Marbury sought to claim the office by taking James Madison to the Supreme Court.

In *Marbury* v. *Madison*, Marshall, now chief justice, wrote that the Court could not legally order Marbury's commission to be delivered, though the Judiciary Act of 1789 said it possessed that right. By declaring that portion of the law invalid, the Court established its power to declare laws of Congress unconstitutional. Said Marshall, " . . . the theory of every government must be that an act of the legislature, repugnant to the Constitution, is void." Today, the power of judicial review is a basic part of the American constitutional system.

HOW THE COURT SYSTEM IS ORGANIZED

Another major aspect in understanding the Court involves its organization. Today's federal court system includes dis-

John Marshall, who served as Chief Justice from 1801 to 1835, led the Supreme Court in many decisions that shaped the nation's destiny.

trict courts, courts of appeals, and the United States Supreme Court. In general, these courts handle the following:

- Criminal and civil cases that involve constitutional or federal law
- Cases in which the United States government is one of the parties
- Cases between individuals or groups from different states
- Cases involving other countries or their citizens.

District courts are the first federal courts to try most cases involving a violation of federal law. Thus, they are federal courts of "original jurisdiction." The United States and its possessions contain ninety-five district courts. If a party to a case heard in a district court does not agree with that court's decision, he or she can appeal to a federal court of appeals. These courts also review decisions made by federal agencies, including the Securities and Exchange Commission and the National Regulations Board. The United States is sectioned into thirteen circuits or regions, each containing a court of appeals.

In addition to district courts and courts of appeal, the United States federal judicial system also includes several specialized courts. The United States Claims Court tries cases involving claims against the federal government. Taxpayers ordered to pay more federal income tax can appeal to the Tax Court of the United States. Disputes involving import duties can reach settlement in the Court of International Trade. Legal offenses involving members of the armed forces can be tried first in courts-martial and on appeal in the Court of Military Appeals.

The final arbiter of judicial questions, the Supreme Court of the United States, hears cases from federal courts of appeal or from the highest court within a state. The judicial system of each state is also headed by a supreme court. In some cases the highest state court is called a court of appeal.

THE SUPREME
COURT'S APPELLATE
JURISDICTION

The vast majority of Supreme Court cases are appellate cases. This means that a party to a case dissatisfied with the decision of the federal courts of appeal or the specialized courts in the federal system can appeal to the Supreme Court. Cases from a state's highest court can be appealed to the Supreme Court only if they involve claims concerning federal law or the Constitution. Appeals from decisions of the state's highest court can go only to the Supreme Court, never to federal courts of appeals or district courts.

Most of the appellate cases come to the Supreme Court as petitions for *writ of certiorari*, a written order calling the case up from a lower court for review. In this instance, the petition for *certiorari* is submitted by an attorney along with a *brief*, a document setting out the facts of the case and the legal arguments in support of the represented party. If the Court decides the case is one it should consider, it will issue a writ ordering the lower court to prepare the record of the case and send it to the Supreme Court for review. From there the Court will examine the facts of the case and issue its decision.

The Court hears only a small proportion of the cases it is asked to review. Out of some 5,000 appeals filed with the Court annually, it writes opinions for approximately 180. Within the entire federal judicial system the court hears fewer than 1 percent of cases appealed from the district courts. Though this book focuses on the Supreme Court, the reader should also keep in mind that the lower courts can and do carve out important policies in deciding cases. Given the volume of cases handled every year by the lower courts of our federal judicial system, we should certainly not think that nothing of any consequence happens at this level.

HOW THE COURT
MAKES DECISIONS

The Constitution permits Congress to decide the number of justices of the Supreme Court. Since 1869, the Court has consisted of eight associate justices and one chief justice. In making decisions, the chief justice and associate justices are on equal ground. The chief justice's vote carries no more weight than those of associate justices. Justices hold their positions for life, unlike the president and legislators who are responsible from term to term to voters at the polls.

The Court sits in session thirty-six weeks per year, from the first Monday in October until the end of June. Situated in Washington, D.C., the Court did not move into its own building until 1935. Commonly referred to as a "marble palace," the Supreme Court building covers a square block located across the street from the U.S. Capitol building. Sessions take place in a courtroom seating three hundred people. Here the justices sit according to seniority behind a long bench at the front of the room. The chief justice sits in the center, the senior associate justice to the chief justice's right, the second-ranking associate justice on the left, and the other associate justices seated alternately in order of seniority.

The justices make their decision in a case after they have considered written and oral arguments from each side. Oral arguments are usually scheduled Monday through Wednesday from 10 A.M. to noon and from 1 P.M. until 3 P.M. Here the two opposing attorneys present their arguments to the justices. An oral argument must be presented within thirty minutes, although the Court may decide that more time is necessary. During this session, the justices can interrupt the attorney and ask questions. This is the only stage in the litigation procedure that allows for interaction with the justices and is considered very important.

The Court holds conference sessions during weeks when

arguments have been heard. These sessions are entirely private with no journalists or other observers allowed. After a preliminary discussion of each case, the chief justice then offers an opinion. Each associate justice follows with his or her opinion in descending order of seniority. Six members of the Court must be present when deciding a case. Most of the time all nine justices are present so there is seldom any difficulty in obtaining a quorum. Decisions are finalized by majority vote, but in case of a tie the lower-court decision is upheld.

After the justices have expressed their opinions in conference, they will vote on the decision. If the chief justice votes with the majority, he will assign the writing of the opinion either to himself or to another justice who voted with the majority. If the chief justice voted with the minority, then the senior associate justice in the majority assigns the opinion.

Once the conference has adjourned, the justice chosen to write the opinion begins the first draft. When completed, the opinion circulates to justices in the majority group and the minority group. This stage is considered a bargaining process whereby the opinion writer seeks to persuade justices in the minority to change votes and to keep the majority group intact. During this stage the wording of the opinion may be changed as a compromise to other justices or to obtain another justice's support. A court deeply divided makes it hard to attain a clear and coherent opinion. In extreme cases it may result in a shift in votes or even some other justice's opinion becoming the Court's official ruling.

Most of the time, though, majority support is obtained and a single opinion rendered. In some cases the Court does arrive at a decision unanimously, although the possibility of this happening is rare. Justices who disagree with the Court's opinion can write a dissenting opinion. If more than one justice dissents, each may write an opinion or else join in a single opinion. Sometimes a justice agrees with the majority decision but will have a different reason for coming to that conclusion. In this case, a justice will write what is called a concurring opinion.

The Supreme Court decisions can have far-reaching effects. Not only must lower courts abide by these decisions, the Supreme Court itself infrequently goes against its previous rulings. This doctrine of adhering to principles of law established in earlier decisions is referred to as *precedent*. In rare instances where the Court believes it has erred in an earlier decision, it is obliged to overrule that decision. For example, in 1954, in *Brown* v. *Board of Education*, the Court ruled "separate but equal" facilities for blacks unconstitutional. The decision overruled a decision the Court had made sixty years earlier that sanctioned segregation practices in the South. This ruling, in *Plessy* v. *Ferguson* (1896), is considered the Court's most tragic and mistaken decision.

THE COURT
AS POLICY-MAKER

In deciding the outcome of major legal battles like those mentioned above, the Supreme Court plays a role in setting government policy. Such important policy issues as racial equality, abortion rights, freedom of speech and the press, and criminal rights all come before the Court in the form of legal disputes. The Court derives its power to make policy by interpreting laws to resolve these disputes. Initially, the Court's decision becomes policy for the specific litigants in the case decided. In a broader sense, the Court's interpretation of the laws extends to the entire lower court system.

This "trickle-down" effect of Court policies into the legal mainstream can have major repercussions. In a democracy, matters of public policy are normally left to those elected to public office by the American people, not to judges appointed for life. Yet, as Chapter Three will demonstrate, the Court can and does chart the course for many public policy issues.

The role of the Supreme Court and the way it interprets the laws change occasionally. These changes reflect the political, social, and economic beliefs of its members and, to some extent, the societal conditions of the time. In the Court's earliest days it concerned itself with the balance of authority between federal and state government. During the period from 1865 to 1937, the Court shifted its emphasis from federalism to economic regulation. This change was brought on by a growing number of national and state laws aimed at monitoring business activities. A major concern of the Court since 1937 has been the protection of the civil rights and liberties of U.S. citizens. The effect that the Court has had in each of these areas is our next topic.

The Court's Impact

3

One hundred and fifty years ago the French scholar Alexis de Toqueville observed that "scarcely any political question arises in the United States that is not resolved sooner or later into a judicial question." These words remain just as true in contemporary times. Many important issues, including government regulation of business and industry, restrictions on freedom of the press, and racial discrimination, continue to pass through the Supreme Court in the form of legal questions. As a result, the Supreme Court—as the final arbiter of judicial questions—is eventually brought into many of the great controversies that have shaped our nation.

FEDERALISM

During different periods of the Court's history it has addressed major issues of public policy. One issue that has had a major impact in Amerian history concerns federalism, or the legal relationship between the national government and state governments. Under Chief Justice John Marshall, the Court gave strong support to the federal government. This was especially evident in the Court's restricting state policies that interfered with Congress's ability to control interstate commerce (business transactions between people or organizations in different states).

In *Gibbons* v. *Ogden* (1824), the Court outlawed a steamboat monopoly in New York State because it impinged upon interstate navigation. The main issue in the case concerned whether the state government or the federal government should control interstate commerce. In his opinion, Chief Justice Marshall proclaimed that only Congress had the authority "to regulate Commerce among the several states," no matter how indirect that activity might be.

The decision had a monumental effect on the country's transportation system. Not only could more steamboats operate and Americans find it easier to get to new parts of the country, it also signaled the dawn of a new railroad system. With state laws now powerless to restrict interstate commerce, railway lines could spread across the nation undeterred by state railways or the individual states.

A century later, in the case of *Baldwin* v. *Seelig*, the Supreme Court reaffirmed the *Ogden* decision by barring any acts of state protectionism not authorized by Congress. This mainly concerned state laws restricting out-of-state businesses from conducting business in-state. In the Court's leading opinion, Justice Benjamin Cardozo wrote that "the

The decision in Gibbons *v.* Ogden *was instrumental in the development of transportation and commerce in the young United States. This landmark ruling made it possible for steamboats, and later rail lines, to cross state boundaries without restriction by state governments.*

BOSTON AND NEW YORK,

VIA NEWPORT AND FALL RIVER.

BAY STATE LINE.

This Route is by steamer from New York to Fall River, 180 miles, and thence by railroad, 53 miles, (one hour and forty minutes,) to Boston. On this route are the well-known steamers

EMPIRE STATE,	1650 tons burthen,	Capt. Benjamin Brayton,
BAY STATE,	1600 " "	" William Brown,
STATE OF MAINE,		" Thomas Jewitt.

The Company is also building a new steamer, which will be the largest steamboat afloat. She will measure nearly 2300 tons,—length 345 feet.—breadth of beam, hull 45 feet and over guards 82 feet,—depth of hold 15 feet. She will have 112 state-rooms, and sleeping accommodations for nearly twice the number that either the other boats can accommodate. She will be on the Line early in the summer.

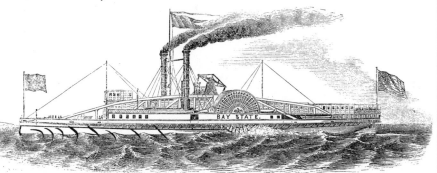

These Boats are not surpassed, either in strength or safety, by any other boats ever constructed, and are elegantly and substantially fitted up with everything calculated to contribute to the ease, comfort and safety of travelers. One of them leaves New York every afternoon, (Sunday excepted,) at 5 o'clock P. M., (at 4 o'clock in the winter months,) and arrives at Fall River at an early hour in the morning, whence, after a comfortable night's rest, the traveler may proceed direct to Boston by steamboat train.

Passengers from Boston to New York take the steamboat train which leaves the Old Colony Railroad Depot, Boston, every afternoon, (Sundays excepted,) for Fall River, arriving at the latter place in time for an early supper on board one of the above boats, which starts for New York immediately on arrival of the train.

Providence passengers are forwarded to and from Fall River by steamers Bradford Durfee or Canonicus.

For all further particulars see bills and advertisements of the day.

Wm. BORDEN, Agent,

70 & 71 WEST STREET, NEW YORK.

Constitution was framed upon the theory that the peoples of the several states must sink or swim together, and that in the long run prosperity and salvation are in union not division."

Such decisions have had a profound effect not only on our history but also on the individuals within the cases. For example, as a result of the *Gibbons* v. *Ogden* ruling, Aaron Ogden—whose monopoly was voided by the Court—went bankrupt, while steamboat-line owner Thomas Gibbons—whose business prospered once commerce restrictions between states were lifted—died a millionaire.

In modern times the Court has continued to uphold the notion of a strong national government. In 1978, the Supreme Court held that Alaska could not require that the state's oil industry employers hire Alaskans first. This practice, reasoned the Court, discriminated against persons from other states. In another instance, Alaska had a plan to share with its citizens the monies from the oil fields at Prudhoe Bay. Under the plan, the amount of dividends a resident would receive would be based on the length of time the person had lived in the state. The Supreme Court in 1982 ruled the plan unconstitutional, stating it discriminated against recent residents of the state by creating different degrees of citizenship based on length of residence.

The federal government's commerce power has not totally overwhelmed the states, however. Giving the states leeway allows them the latitude to create new jobs, choose different ways to supply energy, and design their own land-zoning, taxation, and social services programs. Included among the many privileges extended to the state governments is the power to provide tuition and admission preferences to state residents attending state universities. States also have the power to engage in some areas of economic regulation. For example, in *Pacific Gas & Electric Company* v. *California Energy Commission* (1983), the Court held that states have the power to decide, on economic grounds, the future of nuclear power within their boundaries. All these areas have a direct effect upon each state resident.

CIVIL RIGHTS

Another major area where Supreme Court decisions have had a direct impact on American life is civil rights, through Court rulings focusing on the guarantees of freedom of expression and religion, the rights of criminal defendants, racial minorities, and other disadvantaged groups. Two significant areas that demonstrate some aspects of the Court's influence are freedom of expression and civil rights for blacks.

Freedom of Expression

More than any other branch of government, the Supreme Court has done much to expand the First Amendment's guarantee of freedom of expression. Freedom of expression generally refers to freedom of speech and the press. Freedom of speech is the right of Americans to say publicly or privately what they believe. This extends to all forms of expression, including television, motion pictures, books, newspapers, and radio. Freedom of the press gives Americans the right to publish facts, opinions, and ideas without government or private groups interfering. The term covers the print media and the electronic media (television and radio).

Restrictions on the freedom of expression rights of speech and press usually occur during times of stress, when threats to the nation's security seem grave. During World War I, for example, many Americans regarded the concept of "free speech" as dangerous. The Court too, saw limits to the speech protections provided by the First Amendment. In *Schenck* v. *United States* (1919) the Court ruled that the federal government could prosecute members of the Socialist

Party for mailing leaflets to young American men urging them to resist the draft. Their expressions, held the Court, endangered military recruitment and national security interests.

Since 1919, Court rulings on freedom of speech have been based upon whether the action presented a "clear and present" danger to the nation. Then, in 1951, Congress passed the Smith Act, making it a crime to urge the violent overthrow of the United States government. Both of these policies were tested in the years immediately following World War II in the late forties and fifties.

During that time a number of events took place, creating hostility between communist and noncommunist countries. These included the communist takeovers of Czechoslovakia and China and the detonation of the Soviet Union's first atomic bomb. In addition, the Soviets equipped the North Korean forces that invaded South Korea. The invasion began the Korean War (1950–53).

In the United States, the threat of communism resulted in widespread public hysteria as some Republican politicians, most notably Senator Joseph McCarthy, charged that Communists were occupying positions in the government and infiltrating the military. Threatened by Republican charges that they were being too "soft on communism," the Democratic Party under President Harry Truman realized that it too must toughen its stance or else risk the possibility of losing in forthcoming elections. Consequently, the Justice Department in 1949 indicted eleven members of the American Communist Party for (1) willfully and knowingly conspiring to organize the Communist Party and (2) willfully and knowingly supporting and teaching the duty and necessity of overthrowing the government by force and violence.

After a trial lasting nine months, the Communist leaders were found guilty as charged. The Supreme Court, then headed by Chief Justice Fred Vinson, affirmed these convictions in *Dennis* v. *United States*. In writing the majority opinion, Vinson upheld the Smith Act by stating that it was a crime to advocate the violent overthrow of the United States government or to belong knowingly to a group advocating it.

Since the mid-1950s the courts have become more concerned about personal rights and have thus provided greater protection for freedom of speech. Beginning in 1957 with *Yates* v. *United States* and continuing with other decisions since, the Court has helped protect the rights of persons accused of sympathizing with Communists.

The Court also protected the freedom of speech rights of persons who used "offensive" language to protest the Vietnam War. When Paul Cohen, an opponent of the Vietnam War, entered the Los Angeles Courthouse wearing a jacket bearing a four-letter swear word denouncing the draft, he was arrested and charged with disturbing the peace. In 1971, the Supreme Court reversed Cohen's conviction observing that "one man's vulgarity is another's lyric."

In another freedom of speech case—*Easton* v. *City of Tulsa* (1974), in which a defendant had been cited for contempt of court when he used a slang term for chicken manure in his testimony to describe another person—Justice Lewis Powell commented, "Language likely to offend the sensibility of some listeners is now fairly commonplace in many social gatherings as well as in public performances."

The Court, in addition, has extended "freedom of speech" to include other forms of expression, like the wearing of armbands to protest the Vietnam War. By giving constitutional protections to such modern modes of speech the Court has allowed individuals greater freedom to behave in ways that society at large may find unconventional or distasteful. This judicial tolerance for many forms of expression has also held true in Court rulings focusing on protections for the press.

The Court and the Press: *New York Times Company* v. *United States* (1971) stands as the decision most experts refer to when discussing the Court's expansion of freedom of the press. It began when the *New York Times* secretly obtained a forty-seven-volume Pentagon document outlining the history of the Vietnam War. After reviewing the document, the *Times* believed that the nation should be informed of its contents. On June 13, 1971, it began publishing an analysis of the secret report. Two days later, the Nixon administration, convinced that the publication would harm the United States' position in Vietnam, tried to halt further publication by filing a lawsuit against the *Times*.

In an intense decision, the Supreme Court held that the government had not proved that the publication of the Pentagon papers would endanger national security. In a much quoted concurring opinion, Justice Hugo Black condemned the government's attempts to hold back the information, calling its actions ". . . a flagrant, indefensible and continuing violation of the First Amendment. . . . In my view, far from deserving condemnation for their courageous reporting, *The New York Times* . . . should be commended for serving the purpose that the Founding Fathers saw so clearly. In revealing the workings of the Vietnam War, the newspaper nobly did precisely that which the Founders hoped and trusted they would do." The decision thus expanded the freedom of newspapers and magazines to comment on public issues by limiting the ability of public officials to win legal suits against the press.

Obscenity is another area of expression that deals with both speech and press. In recent years the Court has devoted a great deal of attention to this matter. The term is used to designate materials—written, recorded, and pictorial— that many people may find indecent or offensive. "Obscenity" refers also to language or behavior believed to corrupt public morals. The terms "obscenity" and "pornography" are used interchangeably.

Laws banning obscenity have been difficult to enforce because judges, juries, and the public all may interpret them differently. What some consider obscene may not seem so to others. One group believes that the distribution of obscene materials does, in fact, corrupt public morals. Others are convinced that laws banning obscenity violate the rights of free speech and press guaranteed by the First Amendment.

In 1957 the Supreme Court ruled in the case of *Roth* v. *United States* that freedom of the press does not apply to pornography. The Court went on to provide general guidelines to determine what should be considered obscene. These guidelines were redesigned in *Miller* v. *California* (1973). There, Chief Justice Burger, writing for the majority, reaffirmed the *Roth* ruling's proclamation that obscene materials are not protected by the First Amendment. The *Miller* case, however, went a step beyond the guidelines by stating that pornography cases should be decided by trial courts on the basis of individual community standards, not national ones.

Overall Effect: Historians conclude that the Court's expansion of free expression has had a modest influence in shaping society's ideas and attitudes. Although some groups, such as booksellers, critics of the government, journalists, and dissenters against American foreign policy, have had more freedom because of the Court's decisions, those rights are limited by other forces in society. According to law author Lawrence Baum, the private sector stands as the biggest obstacle to Court rulings permitting freedom of expression.

People may not express themselves because they fear their friends or neighbors will criticize them or because they may be fired. It is, therefore, difficult to discuss with accuracy the impact of the Court's policies. Says Baum, "The Court's pronouncements on freedom of expression might have an indirect impact on the private sector by building public support for free expression, but there is little evidence of such an effect."

It is possible, nevertheless, to pinpoint some specific

examples of the Court's influence in this area. In the area of speech, the Court may have encouraged student uprisings by protecting the rights of persons who opposed the Vietnam War. According to Baum, two cases in particular, *Oestereich* v. *Selective Service System* (1968) and *Gutknecht* v. *United States* (1970), may have contributed to the growth of the antiwar movement by the Court's forbidding the Selective Service System to strike back at those opposed to the war.

The Court's ruling in *New York Times Company* v. *United States* and other decisions allowing the press to expose classified government materials has resulted in more than sixteen years of hostilities between the presidency and the press. A recent sampling of presidential disapproval of these rulings came in October, 1983 when the United States invaded the Caribbean island of Grenada. To its shock, the news media was not given any prior warning of the invasion nor was it allowed on the island for the first two days. The administration's message to the news media: if you can't be trusted, you won't be informed.

In the area of obscenity, Court rulings have been complicated and contradictory. Although the Court has restricted free expression in this area, its guidelines defining obscenity indicate that only the "most offensive" material can be held obscene. This vagueness in terminology has made it difficult to successfully prosecute for obscenity. The result has been a general trend toward freer publication and distribution of materials containing provocative matter.

Civil Rights and Racial Equality

Another area where the Court's influence has been important is in protecting the rights of minorities. The United States contains many minority groups—blacks, Jews, Asian-Americans, European immigrants, Spanish-speaking Americans, and American Indians. Members of these groups have often been denied an equal opportunity for economic, political, or social advancement.

The largest minority group, black Americans, has been denied civil rights more than any other group. Beginning in 1857, the Supreme Court in *Dred Scott* v. *Sanford* held that black slaves could never be citizens because they were "not part of the American people." In the Court's opinion, Chief Justice Taney, writing for seven of the nine justices, denied blacks any constitutional rights by relegating them to "articles of merchandise."

Few Supreme Court opinions have stirred as much fervor among the American public. Southerners hailed it as a victory while northern abolitionists reacted with unprecedented bitterness. The effect of the ruling contributed to destroying the delicate balance between the two opposing sides, which eventually led to civil war.

Following the Civil War, blacks began making significant gains. With Congress' adoption of the Thirteenth Amendment, abolishing slavery, in 1865, and the Fourteenth Amendment in 1868, making the former slaves citizens, it appeared that the government was, at last, granting blacks equal protection under the law.

Then, some thirty years later, the Supreme Court dealt another legal blow. In the 1896 case of *Plessy* v. *Ferguson*, the Court upheld a Louisiana law requiring separate but equal accommodations for blacks and whites in railroad cars. For the next fifty years, several southern states used the "separate but equal" rule to segregate blacks in public schools and in other public establishments.

Since the 1940s, the general thrust of the Court's policies in the areas of political, social, and economic advancement for blacks has been favorable. The high point came in 1954 with *Brown* v. *Board of Education*. In this case, the Court ruled segregation in public schools unconstitutional. The *Brown* decision began a new era of Court policy designed to improve the status of blacks.

The most visible area of improvement has been in the growth of black political power in the past thirty years. With the increase of registered black voters, a strong mi-

*This elementary school was one of the first
to integrate in* 1954, *following the*
Brown *v.* Board of Education *decision
ruling school segregation unconstitutional.*

nority constituency has developed. In 1960, the U.S. Bureau of the Census reported 29 percent of the nonwhite residents in eleven states were registered voters. By 1982, that figure had risen to 57 percent.

This rise in black voters is attributed partly to civil rights laws of the fifties and sixties and also to the civil rights movement of the same period. Each encouraged and supported the growth in number of black elected officials, which rose from 100 in 1964 to 5,100 in 1982. Many observers believe, however, that both elements had a direct connection with Supreme Court decisions. If the Court had not ruled on the *Brown* decision, Congress might not have had the incentive to act against segregation by means of civil rights legislation.

Similarly, the civil rights movement gained momentum with the Court's antidiscrimination rulings. The movement began in the mid-fifties soon after the Court's *Brown* ruling. In 1957, Congress passed the first federal civil rights bill setting up a Commission on Civil Rights to investigate charges of denial of those rights. More coal was added to the movement's fire in 1964 with the Court's decision in *Heart of Atlanta Motel* v. *United States*. Here the Court held that the 1964 Civil Rights Act, banning racial discrimination in all public accommodations, is constitutional. Next, in 1969, the Court departed from the *Brown* ruling's "all deliberate speed" doctrine, which allowed schools to desegregate at their own pace, and ordered the desegregation of all school systems "at once." In both these cases the Court helped support the development of the civil rights movement by ensuring constitutional protections for its constituents.

Impact of Court's Segregation Rulings: Because of several Supreme Court rulings, segregation practices in public accommodations have to a large degree been eliminated. Separate school systems, restaurants, motels, and other public accommodations for blacks no longer exist. Nevertheless, education remains virtually segregated in much of the United States. In 1980, 18 percent of nonwhite public school children attended schools where only 1 percent of the enrollment was white.

Experts cite racial discrimination in housing as one reason for the continuing segregation. Despite a 1968 Supreme Court ruling that prohibits discrimination in the sale or rental of all housing, blacks and other minorities still remain largely segregated from white neighborhoods. This gives evidence of how little influence the Court has had in both the private and public sectors in meeting desegregation goals.

One reason for this applies to the relationship between the Court and the general public. A Court order to desegregate schools may be blunted when white parents opposed to the ruling resist by moving to another school district or by enrolling their children in private schools. In the same light, whites may refuse to live in the same neighborhoods as blacks or else move from a neighborhood where a black family has purchased a house.

The Court has no control over these circumstances. Limitations such as these must therefore be weighed against the Court's strengths. Court decisions have not entirely eliminated discrimination against blacks, but they have helped to bring about improvement in the status of blacks. Rulings to abolish certain practices in society do not guarantee that they will disappear.

Yet, Supreme Court decisions can contribute to the process of change in society. The Court's decisions, according to observers, help create the conditions for action by other institutions. Its rulings earmark certain issues so that public policy-makers and the general public will consider them. The Court makes valid efforts to achieve specific rights and, by doing so, provides the incentive for legal and political action. Court decisions can change the position of various groups or social movements, sometimes negatively, sometimes positively.

The following chapters will examine the individuals and issues behind Supreme Court decisions during the past three decades, beginning with the Warren Court. An exploration of how the Court's direction developed during this time is important in understanding the present Court's future course.

The Warren Court

4

The Court of Earl Warren brought about a revolution in American justice. During the chief justice's tenure, 1953 to 1968, the Supreme Court set America on a new path in race relations by ruling against discrimination. It changed the character of American politics, establishing the rule that all citizens must be represented equally in state legislatures and in the U.S. Congress. The Court wrote what amounted to a new constitutional code of criminal law, changing the entire process of law enforcement, from investigation to arrest to trial. Without a doubt, the changes made by the Warren Court in the area of civil liberties stand unprecedented in the history of the Supreme Court.

Observers attribute the many monumental strides made by the Court in part to Earl Warren himself. Considered one of the Supreme Court's greatest chief justices, Warren's sense of history, foresight, understanding of people, and outstanding leadership qualities all combined to help convert into law the Court's liberal agenda. Yet as experts point out, Warren's success as a chief justice stands as only one reason for the Court's large role in shaping the nation's destiny. Without other justices on the Court—most notably Hugo Black, William O. Douglas, and William Brennan, in addition to new appointments made in the early 1960s—the votes might not have existed for many of the following changes to occur.

The Warren Court gave new meaning to the Bill of Rights, the first ten amendments to the Constitution originally established to guarantee certain individual liberties against the power of the federal government. State governments, until the passage of the Fourteenth Amendment in 1868, had the option of ignoring these rights. The amendment changed that balance of power by stating in part that no state shall "deprive any person of life, liberty, or property without due process of law."

The term "due process of law" has long been a topic of intense judicial debate. Some law experts argue that the amendment, created following the Civil War, was intended solely to add constitutional strength to laws giving blacks the same judicial benefits as whites. Justice Black, who served on the Court from 1937 to 1971, believed the amendment's framers intended much more. He argued that the due process clause "incorporated," or took on, the entire Bill of Rights, making those rights enforceable on the states. It took him almost twenty years to convince his colleagues to accept his views. Finally, in the early 1960s, with the Warren Court firmly in place, Black's incorporation theory began to take hold.

As a result of several Warren Court decisions (some discussed later in this chapter), virtually all of the Bill of Rights has become the state as well as the federal process due all Americans. Now states are required to enforce the entire First Amendment, the Fourth's guarantee against unreasonable searches and seizures, the Fifth's privilege against self-incrimination, and the Sixth's right to counsel and trial by jury.

DESEGREGATING AMERICA

The Warren Court Revolution began after an eleven-year-old black girl named Linda Brown tried to enroll in an all-white public school in Topeka, Kansas. When her request was denied, her family brought a lawsuit challenging Topeka's segregation law permitting separate sets of schools for black and white students. The law resulted from the 1896 Supreme Court ruling *Plessy* v. *Ferguson*, which upheld "separate but equal" accommodations for blacks and whites.

After losing in the lower courts, *Brown* v. *Board of Education* was appealed to the United States Supreme Court. The Court agreed to hear the case and in 1954 ruled in *Brown* v. *Board of Education* that segregation in public schools was unconstitutional. Calling segregated schools *inherently* unequal, the Court unanimously voted to abolish the separate but equal doctrine.

In writing his most famous opinion for the Court, Warren said, "Today education is perhaps the most important function of state and local governments. . . . Such an opportunity where the state had undertaken to provide it must be made on all equal terms. We come then to the question presented: Does segregation of children in public schools solely on the basis of race, even though the physical facilities and other 'tangibles' may be equal, deprive the children of the minority group of equal educational opportunities? We believe that it does."

Subsequent opinions soon followed, underscoring the enduring nature of this new constitutional doctrine. In *Watson* v. *Memphis*, the Court struck down segregation in public parks, in *Holmes* v. *City of Atlanta* it struck down segregation in public golf courses and other recreational facilities, and in *Turner* v. *Memphis* it called for an end to segregation in airports. The Court continued its pattern in other civil rights cases. In *Gomillion* v. *Lightfoot* (1960), it outlawed the practice of gerrymandering, a method of determining voting districts which had long been used to lessen the effect of black votes. It also invalidated state laws forbidding interracial marriages in *Loving* v. *Virginia* (1967).

The Warren Court in the 1950s began a constitutional revolution in the area of civil rights. The influence of the

Brown decision was so far-reaching and public reaction to it so emotional that it tended to dominate all references to the Court during its first decade.

CONTROVERSIAL DECISIONS

The tension created by the Court's segregation rulings was intensified by others decided in the late 1950s. In 1951, the Court, under Chief Justice Fred Vinson, had ruled in *Dennis* v. *United States* that leaders of the U.S. Communist Party could face prosecution for supporting the violent overthrow of the federal government. But on June 17, 1957, the Warren Court in *Yates* v. *United States* devised strict guidelines making it almost impossible to successfully prosecute under the same charge. On the same day, the Court reversed the conviction for contempt of Congress of an individual who had refused to answer questions from the House Un-American Activities Committee about members of the Communist Party. These two rulings incited anger from conservative critics who blasted the Court for sympathizing with Communists. The critics thus labeled June 17, 1957, "Red Monday."

Next, the Court, in *Mallory* v. *United States*, unanimously overturned a man's conviction for rape, citing that at the time of arrest the police did not inform him of his Fifth Amendment right to remain silent. Conservative feathers were again ruffled when in 1958 the Court struck down Alabama's attempts to force the National Association for the Advancement of Colored People (NAACP) to disclose its membership lists.

Public and political criticism of the Court intensified as a result. Southerners, dissatisfied over the desegregation rulings, joined those critical of the antisubversive rulings, escalating hostility toward the Court to a point unmatched in this century. This prompted Congress to propose legislation—which later failed—withdrawing the Court's jurisdiction over any matters concerning the rights of allegedly subversive persons. The Court continued throughout the sixties to uphold individual claims against the government claims of national security.

EQUAL
REPRESENTATION

In 1962, the Court again initiated widespread reform measures, this time in the area of voting rights. In *Baker* v. *Carr*, it ruled that states must redraw the boundary lines of their congressional districts. During the 1950s and early 1960s rural voters in many states elected far more lawmakers to Congress and state legislatures than did city dwellers. In Vermont, for example, one representative spoke for 49 persons while another spoke for 33,155. A mere 9½ percent of the population in Connecticut elected a majority of state representatives. And in Colorado, the state legislature gave Denver $2.3 million a year in school aid for 90,000 children and $2.4 million a year to a semirural county with 18,000 pupils.

Tennessee's constitution stated that electoral districts should be redrawn every ten years to compensate for any shift in population. Yet the state legislature had not passed a redistricting law since 1901. To show discontent Charles Baker and nine other qualified voters filed suit against Tennessee's Secretary of State Joe C. Carr. After the lower court dismissed *Baker* v. *Carr*, the Supreme Court accepted it.

Justice Brennan spoke for the majority, stating that if a state lets one person's vote count more than another's because they live in different districts, that state denies its citizens equal protection of the law. In another related case, *Gray* v. *Sanders*, Justice Douglas wrote that the promise of political equality as stated in the Constitution meant "one person, one vote." Because of these rulings, political power in Congress and in state legislatures was redistributed equally. Earl Warren considered *Baker* v. *Carr* the most important decision made while he served as chief justice.

CRIMINAL LAW CASES

The Warren Court also dramatically changed procedures followed by the states in dealing with criminal defendants. By Warren's retirement, the Court had established new policies to deal with searches and seizures, police investigation procedures, and fair trial practices. Although the court decided dozens of these cases, among the more far-reaching were *Mapp* v. *Ohio*, *Gideon* v. *Wainwright* and *Miranda* v. *Arizona*.

The Court, in *Mapp* v. *Ohio*, ordered all states to obey the "exclusionary rule" established in a 1949 decision. Based on the Fourth Amendment, the rule excludes from trials any evidence that the police seize illegally. The case revolved around a Cleveland, Ohio, homeowner named Dollree Mapp. In 1957, police broke into her house and seized materials considered obscene by Ohio law. A search warrant was never produced. After battling the case out in the lower courts, the Supreme Court accepted the case on appeal. Ruling that Mapp's Fourth Amendment and Fourteenth Amendment's due process and equal protection rights had been violated, Justice Thomas C. Clark declared: "We hold that all evidence obtained by illegal searches and seizures in violation of the Constitution is, by the same authority, inadmissible in a state court."

As a result of the decision made in *Mapp* v. *Ohio*, law enforcement officials can only conduct a search and seize evidence if a judge has issued them a warrant. Otherwise, even if illegally seized evidence shows guilt, the defendant may be freed because the police have violated his or her constitutional rights.

In another case expanding the rights of criminal defendants, the Court, in *Gideon* v. *Wainwright* (1963), established the Sixth Amendment's right to counsel in state trials. Prior to this ruling the right to have a lawyer to assist in one's defense applied only to federal law. The *Gideon* decision called this practice unconstitutional, ruling that poor defendants must be provided a lawyer when they go to trial in felony cases in state courts. The case focused on defendant Clarence Earl Gideon, who had been charged with "breaking and entering" in Panama City, Florida. Unable to pay for a lawyer, Gideon was forced to defend himself and was subsequently found guilty, receiving a sentence of five years in state prison.

The Supreme Court announced that it would hear Gideon's case, after reading a five-page *writ of certiorari* the defendant had composed from his prison cell. Justice Black—who had dissented twenty years earlier in a similar case, *Betts* v. *Brady* (upholding the conviction of a jobless Maryland farmhand who had been too poor to hire a lawyer—triumphantly announced the decision in *Gideon*.

Gideon's experience, said Black, raised the question of "the rightness of a case we decided twenty-one years ago, Betts against Brady. When we granted certiorari in this case, we asked the lawyers on both sides to argue to us whether we should reconsider that case. We do reconsider Betts and Brady, and we reach an opposite conclusion. . . . Any person held in Court who is too poor to hire a lawyer, cannot be assured a fair trial unless counsel is provided for him." After the decision was announced, Clarence Gideon received a new trial in Florida. This time, with the assistance of a state-appointed lawyer, he was declared innocent of breaking and entering charges.

In *Miranda* v. *Arizona*, the Supreme Court went a step further by ruling that police officers must advise suspects taken into custody of their constitutional rights, one of which is to have a lawyer present during questioning. Suspects must also be advised that they have a right to remain silent and that any statement they make may be used in court. Also, if they cannot afford a lawyer, one will be appointed to them at state expense.

The background of this case concerned Ernest Miranda, arrested and convicted of the kidnapping and rape of an eighteen-year-old woman in Phoenix, Arizona. When Miranda was taken into custody, police did not inform him of his right to remain silent and to seek counsel. During his interrogation he signed a statement confessing to the crime. The evidence was used subsequently in his trial. Miranda was convicted and sentenced to thirty years in prison. After he again lost his case in the Arizona Supreme Court, the United States Supreme Court accepted it on appeal.

In a 5 to 4 vote, the Court held in 1966 that Miranda's confession had been obtained in violation of the Fifth Amendment's protection against self-incrimination. Speaking for the majority, Chief Justice Warren said, " . . . it is clear that Miranda was not in any way apprised of his right to consult with an attorney and to have one present during the interrogation, nor was his right not to be compelled to incriminate himself effectively protected in any manner. Without these warnings the statements were inadmissible." In the same opinion the Court devised a series of warnings for police to read to suspects prior to arrest.

The American public responded to these decisions, particularly *Mapp* and *Miranda*, with mixed emotions. Many felt that the rulings would not only increase the crime rate but would also make it difficult for police to enforce the laws. Law enforcement officials, in particular, resented the Court's efforts to put constraints on investigation procedures.

Studies conducted following the *Miranda* decision found that, overall, police have had little difficulty in carrying out the decision. As one public defender noted in Lawrence Baum's book *The Supreme Court*, "Police love the Miranda decision. They speed-read the suspect his rights and tell

Ernesto Miranda (right), shown here with attorney John J. Flynn, became a household name in 1966 when the Supreme Court ruled that the police must inform a suspect of his constitutional right to remain silent, thereby instituting the famous "Miranda warning."

him to fill in and sign a printed waiver form. He's frightened; he doesn't understand what was read to him; he's afraid he'll look guilty if he doesn't sign; he signs and school's out. The signed waiver is almost impossible for the defense to overcome."

Up until the early 1980s the *Mapp* and *Miranda* rulings remained unchanged. As Chapter Six will discuss, the Burger Court recently weakened the rulings as a result of two decisions. The *Gideon* ruling remains intact.

THE SEPARATION OF CHURCH AND STATE

The Warren Court is remembered for any number of reasons, yet for many Americans, it is most distinctly identified as the Court that put an end to prayer in public school. Among the Court's most highly publicized cases, *Engel* v. *Vitale* generated nearly as much discussion, criticism, and controversy as the school desegregation and criminal law decisions. In this case the Court was called upon to interpret the opening language of the First Amendment: "Congress shall make no law respecting an *establishment* of religion, or prohibiting the *free exercise* of . . ."

It began in 1958 when the New York State Board of Regents composed a twenty-two-word prayer, which was adopted by a Long Island public school district. Every morning the students and teachers of the Herricks school district would recite the prayer, which read: "Almighty God, we acknowledge our dependence upon Thee, and we beg Thy blessings upon us, our parents, our teachers and our country."

A group of parents whose children attended the public school protested the prayer, stating that it violated the First Amendment's establishment clause, which was intended to separate activities between church and state. They brought suit against the Herricks school board, stating that "if the

*In a scene from the past, first graders in a
South Carolina school share a moment of silent
prayer, before the Supreme Court declared
prayer in the public schools unconstitutional.*

state could tell us what to pray and when to pray and how to pray, there was no stopping." On the other side, lawyers argued that the school board was exercising its freedom of religious expression. Four years later, the issue exploded with the Supreme Court decision in *Engel* v. *Vitale*. Here the Court declared it unconstitutional for children to recite prayers in the Herricks system or in any public school system in America.

Justice Black, who wrote the majority opinion, rejected criticism that banning school prayer was hostile "toward religion or toward prayer." He wrote, "Nothing . . . could be more wrong. [The framers of the Bill of Rights] knew that the First Amendment . . . was written to quiet well-justified fears which nearly all of them felt arising out of an awareness that governments of the past had shackled men's tongues to make them speak only the religious thoughts that government wanted them to speak and to pray only to the God that government wanted them to pray to." He continued, saying it was "Neither sacrilegious nor antireligious to say that . . . government . . . should stay out of the business of writing or sanctioning official prayers and leave that purely religious function to the people themselves."

Since the practice of prayer in school at the time was widespread, it is not surprising that the decision met with sharp opposition. Many citizens and politicians vehemently attacked the Court for what they perceived as unbridled activism. One congressman from Georgia complained that the Warren Court had "put the Negroes in the schools—now they put God out of the schools." Another congressman from New York attacked the *Engel* v. *Vitale* ruling as "the most tragic decision in the history of the United States."

President John Kennedy and other politicians and citizens were not as outraged. Kennedy offered this advice, " . . . we have in this decision a very easy remedy and that is to pray ourselves." Senator Philip Hart of Michigan called the decision "right and proper."

Some school districts responded to the ruling by allowing, instead, the recitation of the Lord's prayer, reasoning that since the state didn't write it, it didn't violate Court policy. A year later, in *Abington School District* v. *Schempp*, the Warren Court struck down this new practice pointing out that it violated the Constitution by endorsing religious activity and that it did not matter whether the state had written the prayer.

THE END OF
THE WARREN ERA

In 1968, Earl Warren resigned. President Lyndon Johnson quickly moved to elevate Justice Abe Fortas to the position of chief justice. His attempts proved to be in vain after reports surfaced charging Fortas with unethical conduct while on the Court. After months of Senate confirmation hearings, Fortas resigned from the Court under threat of impeachment. In his letter of resignation, Fortas asserted his innocence, saying he left the Court to avoid placing it under undue stress.

Meanwhile the Republicans had hopes of winning the presidency. They hoped to see their candidate, Richard Nixon, select the new chief justice. Their hopes were given added significance by candidate Nixon's criticism of the Court as a major campaign issue. Charging the Court with "coddling criminals," Nixon promised to appoint justices more sympathetic to conservative views.

The Burger Court

5

After his election victory in 1968, President Richard Nixon nominated the conservative Warren E. Burger as chief justice. The Senate confirmed the sixty-one-year-old Court of Appeals judge almost immediately. With Nixon's additional appointments of other conservatives—Harry A. Blackmun, Lewis F. Powell, Jr., and William H. Rehnquist—Court observers expected to see many of the landmark decisions of the Warren Court overturned. For almost two decades the Court had played a major role in creating a dominant liberal force in American society. Now it seemed a counterrevolution was close at hand.

But by the time Burger had announced his resignation in 1986, this reversal had not occurred. Even with six of its justices appointed by Republican presidents, the Burger Court took a surprisingly moderate course, cutting back in some areas, most notably the rights of the accused, but going even further than the Warren Court in others. The Burger Court, for example, made monumental liberal strides in upholding a woman's right to abortion and in making sex discrimination in state laws unconstitutional.

One reason a counterrevolution did not occur, according to law experts, stemmed from the Burger Court's inability to develop a consistent judicial vision. Where the Warren Court often handed down broad rulings, the Burger justices tended to treat cases as factual disputes. The result: justices issued more separate opinions, and rulings on major issues often ended up with a 5 to 4 vote or with no majority at all. In the words of Justice Powell, the Court operated as "nine one-man law firms." Some experts blamed the chief justice for the Court's drifting, while others believe that it simply lacked members who possessed the intellectual caliber of a Hugo Black or a Felix Frankfurter.

Another part of the answer according to former Supreme Court correspondent Anthony Lewis, lies in the judicial doctrine of *stare decisis*, or adherence to decided cases: "Conservative judges, meaning by that term those who are more cautious in lawmaking, are naturally committed to the doctrine of *stare decisis*. It follows logically that they should respect a precedent once established even though they opposed that result during the process of decision. . . . Very few judges today are prepared to break boldly from prevailing constitutional doctrines." In other words, justices may not like the abortion ruling but nevertheless regard it as established law, thus binding.

Whatever the reason, the story of the Burger Court is one of a Court neither liberal nor conservative but one unpredictable and divided. Lacking a dominant conservative or liberal wing, the Court's moderate members often guided the outcome of decisions. This subsequently shifted the tribunal from its liberal position to the moderate center. Today the Court sits delicately balanced. One or two substitutions could profoundly change the entire character of the group.

THE BURGER COURT
JUSTICES

How the Court evolved to its present state can be better understood by knowing more about its members. In the following portraits each justice, through his or her opinions and dissents, reveals a distinct and dynamic judicial personality. In examining each portrait, keep in mind two important points essential to understanding the Court's possible future direction.

First, with any new appointment to the Court (as in the case of Sandra Day O'Connor) a close look at that individual's views in contrast with those of the departing justice may help predict how dramatically the Court's chemistry will change. Second, although a president may appoint a conservative justice, that individual's views may change while on the Court, as the Supreme Court record of Justice Blackmun demonstrates.

The following portraits are presented within each justice's usual alliance, either conservative, liberal, or moderate.

THE CONSERVATIVES

Warren E. Burger

Chief Justice Burger will probably be best remembered for an opinion that helped end the political career of the president who appointed him to the Court. In the spring of 1974, Special Prosecutor Leon Jaworski ordered President Richard Nixon to hand over tape-recorded conversations linked to the Watergate conspiracy. When Nixon refused, Jaworski took the matter on appeal to the Supreme Court. The Court unanimously ruled in Jaworski's favor.

Writing for the Court, Burger rejected Nixon's assertion that "executive privilege," as stated in Article II of the Constitution, allowed him to retain presidential documents. Instead the Court, guided by Burger's pen, ruled that Nixon had to obey a court order, because no one, not even the president of the United States, is above the law.

Courtly and white-maned, almost regal in appearance, Burger seemed to fit the image of a chief justice. Born in

Minnesota and graduated from St. Paul College of Law, he came to the Supreme Court from the United States Court of Appeals for the District of Columbia. As an Appeals Court judge he had displayed an intolerance toward expanded constitutional rights of persons accused of crimes. Burger's record in this area caught the attention of President Nixon who as a presidential candidate had promised to appoint justices who would take a conservative approach to law enforcement procedures. In 1969, Nixon appointed Burger as the nation's fifteenth chief justice.

While on the Supreme Court, Burger tended to take a conservative view of civil liberties and displayed a strong belief in the importance of maintaining the Constitution's system of separate powers. On this point he argued that the federal courts should try to avoid overruling state courts and legislatures. When the Court in 1982, for example, ruled that states could *not* refuse to educate the children of illegal aliens, Burger—along with William Rehnquist, Byron White, and Sandra Day O'Connor—dissented. Burger wrote, "Were it our business to set the Nation's policy, I would agree without hesitation that it is senseless for an enlightened society to deny any children—including illegal aliens—of any elementary education.

"However, the Constitution does not constitute us as 'Platonic Guardians,' nor does it vest in this Court the authority to strike down laws because they do not meet our standards of desirable social policy, 'wisdom' or 'common sense'. . . . We trespass on the assigned function of the political branches under our structure of limited and separate powers when we assume a policy making role, as the Court does today."

Burger concluded the dissent with a statement reflecting his belief in judicial restraint. "The Constitution does not provide a cure for every social ill, nor does it vest judges with a mandate to try and remedy every problem."

In the area of church and state, Burger consistently held to the notion that government should not compel citizens to act in the name of any religion. On the other hand, he believed the courts should try to "accommodate" the interests of both church and state.

In a 1984 decision which permitted a city government to sponsor a Christmas nativity scene, Burger spoke for the majority. "No significant segment of our society and no institution within it can exist in a vacuum or in total or absolute isolation from all other parts of government. Nor does the Constitution require complete separation of church and state, it affirmatively mandates accommodation, not merely tolerance, of all religions and forbids hostility towards any."

Burger again held to the accommodation theme when in 1985 the Court struck down an Alabama law that permitted a "moment of silence" for voluntary prayer or meditation in public schools. In a dissenting opinion, Burger criticized the majority's reasoning that the Alabama law was equal to creating an established church.

"The law does not remotely threaten religious liberty. . . . It accommodates the purely private, voluntary religious choices of the individual pupils who wish to pray while at the same time creating a time for nonreligious reflection for those who do not choose to pray," wrote Burger. "The statute endorses only the view that the religious observance of others should be tolerated and where possible, accommodated."

In First Amendment cases involving freedom of the press, Burger generally responded favorably to the press's claims. In *Nebraska Press Association* v. *Stuart*, for example, the Court reversed a Nebraska court order barring press coverage of a criminal trial that involved the murders of six family members. The state court, in issuing the order, had concluded that publicity would infringe upon the defendant's right to a fair trial. In his majority opinion, Burger asserted that "prior restraints on speech and publication are the most serious and least tolerable infringement on First Amendment Rights."

By contrast, cases involving criminal rights and the rights of the accused revealed Burger's most conservative views. He argued for cutting back the exclusionary rule which bars from criminal trials any evidence obtained without a search warrant. He said the Court should limit such exclusions in situations where the evidence was necessary to protect the "integrity of the truth-seeking process." And in 1983, Burger voted for a ruling stating that prisoners have no Fourth Amendment rights against unreasonable searches and seizures in their cells.

The chief justice's belief in the limited role the courts should play in deciding certain issues extended to questions concerning the constitutionality of the death penalty. When the Court in 1972 (*Furman* v. *Georgia*), ruled state death penalty laws unconstitutional on the grounds that they violated the Eighth Amendment's decree against "cruel and unusual punishment," Burger dissented. "In our constitutional inquiry we must be divorced from personal feelings as to the morality and efficacy of the death penalty. . . . It is essential to our role as a Court that we do not seize upon the enigmatic character of the guarantee as an invitation to enact our personal predelections into law."

Overall, Burger did not achieve success as a leader. According to critics, he seemed more at ease with the Court's administrative and ceremonial duties than he did with Court decisions. Burger also received criticism for opinions that lacked craftsmanship and for being indecisive during judicial conferences. The chief justice stepped down from his post in June 1986 to organize the bicentennial celebration of the U.S. Constitution, which took place September 17, 1987. On that same day, Warren E. Burger turned eighty.

William H. Rehnquist

Recently appointed as the sixteenth chief justice of the United States, William Rehnquist is considered the Court's most conservative member. Born in Milwaukee, Wisconsin, he went on to graduate first in his class from Stanford University Law School. After receiving his degree, Rehnquist became a law clerk for Justice Robert Jackson of the U.S. Supreme Court. In 1968, he began serving as United States assistant attorney general under the Nixon administration. In this role Rehnquist became known for his unwavering commitment to conservative political ideas. His approach to the law so impressed Nixon that in 1971 the president appointed Rehnquist as an associate justice of the Supreme Court.

Rehnquist is a staunch advocate of judicial restraint. In his view, the Court should leave to elected officials the business of creating social policies. Innovations in American law, he argues, should come from the other branches of government, not from the judiciary. It is Rehnquist's belief that his colleagues impose their own values into readings of the Constitution. Rehnquist does not, for example, believe there exists a specific constitutional guarantee of a right to privacy. Hence, in decisions upholding abortion rights he dissents consistently.

More than any other justice on the Burger Court, Rehnquist believed that the Constitution should be interpreted according to the intentions of its framers. For example, when the Court in 1985 reaffirmed the ban on prayer in public schools, Rehnquist dissented. Urging his colleagues to throw out the standard idea that the First Amendment's establishment clause required a wall of separation between church and state, Rehnquist said, "The Framers created the Establishment Clause to prohibit the designation of any church as a 'national' one . . . to stop the Federal government from asserting a preference for one religious denomination or sect over another."

In keeping with his conservatism, Rehnquist has displayed strong support for law enforcement officials over persons suspected of committing crimes. Believing that Warren Court decisions such as *Miranda* v. *Arizona* and *Mapp* v. *Ohio* have protected suspects at the expense of the public, Rehnquist has set out to overturn or at least modify those rulings.

In 1984, Rehnquist spoke for the Court in a decision introducing a "public safety exception" to the *Miranda* rule, which orders police to read suspects their rights prior to questioning. By upholding the actions of a policeman who asked an armed rape suspect, "Where's the gun?" before advising him of his rights, Rehnquist said the ruling allowed officers "to follow their legitimate instincts when confronting situations presenting a danger to the public."

Rehnquist's strict interpretation of the Constitution is nowhere more evident than in his consistent dissent in decisions upholding civil or individual rights. No other modern justice has favored such narrow restrictions on the Constitution and the Bill of Rights. In case after case, Rehnquist disagrees with rulings to expand remedial procedures for victims of job discrimination, to ban laws that discriminate against women and illegitimate children, to give First Amendment protections to commercial speech (such as advertisements to sell legal or medical services), and to strike down aid to church schools.

For example, when the Court ruled to support the Internal Revenue Service's move to deny tax-exempt status to Bob Jones University because it discriminates against blacks, Rehnquist argued that the questions involved in the case were a matter for Congress, not for the Courts. "I have no disagreement with the Court's findings that there is a strong national policy in this country opposed to racial discrimination. I agree with the Court that Congress has the power to deny [tax-exempt status] to organizations that practice racial discrimination. But as of yet, Congress has failed to do so. Whatever the reasons for the failure, this Court should not legislate for Congress."

Rehnquist is highly admired for his sharp questioning from the bench, his intelligence, and gregariousness. After Reagan announced Rehnquist's nomination, Stanford University law professor Gerald Gunther commented, "You are trading a vote by Burger for a guy who has a far better brain, endless energy and total commitment to the job."

Yet, the new chief justice has in the past been criticized as being closed-minded and too political in trying to persuade the outcome of cases. To be an effective leader on the Court, Rehnquist will have to moderate these ideals to some extent if he expects to win the support of his colleagues. The sixty-three-year-old chief jurist is currently in good health.

Sandra Day O'Connor

Sandra Day O'Connor has always been a pioneer. She graduated from Stanford University Law School in 1952, at a time when women lawyers were considered a rarity. In 1972, she broke ground again, becoming the first woman elected majority leader of the Arizona Senate. Nine years later, on September 25, 1981, O'Connor set her greatest precedent by becoming the first woman in history to serve on the U.S. Supreme Court.

O'Connor replaced less conservative Potter Stewart, who resigned in 1981. In most areas, Stewart took a moderate position, many times acting as the Court's swing vote, siding with the liberals in some instances and with the conservatives in others. O'Connor, on the other hand, has more often voted with the conservative wing, thus shifting the Court's direction to the right.

O'Connor brought a fresh approach and abundant energy to a Court where age and the repetition of issues had taken their toll. This incisive newcomer often adds concurring opinions when she feels the majority has not fully developed its reasoning—or chosen the correct reasoning.

In her first term, O'Connor rebuked Chief Justice Burger for writing a majority opinion that contributed, as she phrased, "to an uncertain jurisprudence." The following term she refused to join a dissent written by Rehnquist. In explaining her reasoning for writing a separate dissenting opinion, she wrote, "Although both the Court and Justice Rehnquist display admirable skills in legal research and analysis of great numbers of musty cases, the results do not significantly further the goal of inquiry. . . ."

Abortion Rights: A classic example of O'Connor's piercing, analytic style occurred in her dissent in a 1983 abortion case, *City of Akron* v. *Akron Center for Reproductive Health.* In this instance the Court struck down a city ordinance imposing restrictions upon women seeking abortions, thus reaffirming the Court's 1973 abortion decision in *Roe* v. *Wade.* However in O'Connor's dissenting opinion, joined by Justices Rehnquist and Byron White, she uncovered a major logical flaw in the *Roe* decision. In short, that decision held that states could restrict abortions only after the point where the fetus could survive outside the mother's body. In 1972 the point of viability (that point after which a fetus could survive on its own) was around twenty-four weeks. After a detailed examination of the *Roe* decision, O'Connor concluded that as a result of scientific advances in prenatal care the logic behind *Roe* had put the decision "on a collision course with itself." Such advances, asserted O'Connor, could place the point of viability much earlier in the pregnancy. Through her ability to focus on precise points of logic, O'Connor had challenged the Court to either rethink its reasoning in Roe or else watch it become scientifically obsolete.

Like Rehnquist, O'Connor shares the view that states should be given more power to govern themselves. Her opinions demonstrate a faith in the political decisions of state officials by urging the Court to allow them more independence. In 1985, she wrote, "State legislative and administrative bodies are not field offices of the national bureaucracy. Nor are they think tanks to which Congress may assign problems for extended study. Instead, each state is sovereign within its own domain, governing its citizens and providing for their general welfare."

Similarly, in the area of First Amendment freedoms, O'Connor has shown reluctance to restrain state or local governments. In a 1983 opinion, the Court ruled that First Amendment protections would not allow a public school board to remove certain books from the school library. O'Connor dissented, stating, "If the school board can set the curriculum, select teachers, and determine initially what books to purchase for the school library, it surely can decide which books to discontinue or remove from the school library."

Sex Discrimination: It's not surprising that as the Court's sole female member, O'Connor's opinions on sex discrimination have drawn particular attention. She has recalled publicly her own victimization. After graduating near the top of her law school class, she could not find a law firm that would hire a woman.

Generally, she supports those who challenge sex discrimination. In 1983, she spoke for the Court's majority when it ruled that the University of Mississippi for Women violated the Constitution by refusing to admit men to its nursing program. And in 1983 she joined Justices Marshall, Brennan, White, and Stevens in ruling that employers could not offer retirement plans giving women retirees smaller monthly payments based on statistical evidence that they live longer than men.

In criminal law cases, O'Connor usually favors police and prosecutors over criminal suspects. Prior to her appointment, the Court ruled in *Robbins* v. *California* that police must first obtain a search warrant before opening a closed container in a car. The ruling was the last opinion written by Justice Potter Stewart, O'Connor's predecessor. Then in June 1982, during her first term, O'Connor voted with the majority to reverse the *Robbins* decision, making it legal for police to search any container in the car, without a search warrant.

During her first five years on the Burger Court, O'Connor repeatedly allied herself with Chief Justice Burger and Justices Rehnquist and Powell. She has become not only the Court's first woman but also this Court's third conservative vote. In replacing a moderate justice with a staunch conservative, President Reagan's first Supreme Court appointment has had a notable impact. At fifty-eight, O'Connor appears in good health.

THE LIBERALS

William J. Brennan

In 1984 the *National Review* magazine observed about the Court's most senior member: "Justice Brennan more than virtually anybody else in public life today has made a difference." A statement of this magnitude coming from one of the country's most conservative publications demonstrates just how respected is the judicial career of Justice William Brennan. For over thirty years Brennan has displayed a deep commitment to civil and individual rights by strongly upholding the notion of a powerful federal court system. He believes this is necessary to protect those rights from being abused by other branches of government and by state courts.

Born in Newark, New Jersey, in 1906, the son of an Irish immigrant and boiler worker, Brennan went on to graduate with honors from the University of Pennsylvania. In 1931 he graduated in the top 10 percent of his Harvard Law School class. Prior to being appointed to the Court, Brennan served on the New Jersey Supreme Court, where he was highly respected and generally considered a liberal.

Appointed to the U.S. Supreme Court in 1956 by President Dwight Eisenhower, Brennan often wrote for the liberal majority of the Warren Court. It was Brennan's controversial opinion in *Baker* v. *Carr* (1962) that ordered state

The justices of the Burger Court:
(from left) Justices Harry Blackmun, Thurgood Marshall,
William Brennan, Chief Justice Warren Burger,
Justices Sandra Day O'Connor, Byron White, Lewis Powell,
William Rehnquist, and John Paul Stevens.

legislatures to reapportion themselves according to population. Four years later he wrote the opinion upholding the Voting Rights Act of 1965, enacted to outlaw literacy tests which had been used in some states as a means to deprive blacks of the right to vote.

After the departure of Justices Hugo Black, William O. Douglas, and Earl Warren from the Court, Justice Brennan found himself in the minority. Now allied with Justice Thurgood Marshall, his role on the Court, according to observers, is less one of persuading other justices than of holding on to majorities that already exist. In 1982, after redrafting an opinion several times to gain the vote of Justice Powell, Brennan wrote for the majority in ruling that Texas could not deny illegal aliens a free public education.

In the decision, which was considered a highly visible liberal victory, Brennan stated that, "The inability to read and write will handicap the individual deprived of a basic education each and every day of his life. The inestimable toll of that deprivation on the social, economic, intellectual, and psychological well-being of the individual, and the obstacles it poses to individual achievement, makes it most difficult to reconcile . . . a status-based denial of basic education with the framework of equality embodied in the Equal Protection Clause."

Brennan views the federal courts as the guardian of the individual against possible mistreatment by state governments or other branches of the federal government. When the Court upheld the warrantless detention of a suspected drug smuggler by U.S. customs agents, Brennan railed at his colleagues in the majority for allowing "such a ring of unbridled authoritarianism surrounding freedom's soil."

The Dealth Penalty: As the Court's strongest opponent of the death penalty, Brennan has consistently held to the view that the practice is incalculably cruel and unusual, thus unconstitutional. On the subject he has written, "The calculated killing of a human being by the state, involves by its very nature, a denial of the executed person's humanity."

According to former law clerks, the conferences with Brennan about death cases are very painful.

Freedom from government interference in one's personal life, the right to privacy, finds its staunchest defender in Brennan. Even though his own religion, Roman Catholicism, would suggest that he would oppose abortion, he sides with a woman's right to choose to have an abortion. He has also written majority opinions denying states the power to restrict contraceptives. "If the right of privacy means anything," Brennan wrote, "it is the right to the individual, married or single, to be free from unwarranted governmental intrusion into matters so fundamentally affecting a person as the decision whether to bear or beget a child."

Brennan suffered a minor stroke in 1979 but otherwise appears healthy. The oldest member of the court remains an optimist. In a recent *New York Times* article, Brennan said, "It's thrilling to be here every day since the day I came. And it'll continue to be exciting and thrilling every day until the day I go. At the same time it's also a very— burden is not the right word—well, maybe let's say that you just always appreciate the significance of what you're called on to do and decide."

Thurgood Marshall

The first black Supreme Court justice was born in Baltimore, Maryland, in 1908, the great-grandson of a slave. Excluded because of his race from the University of Maryland Law School, Marshall attended Howard University, where he graduated first in his class. He left Baltimore in 1936 to become special counsel to the National Association for the Advancement of Colored People (NAACP).

After two years he became director of the NAACP Legal Defense Fund, and for twenty-five years Marshall engineered the legal strategies of the civil rights movement. In 1954, he argued before the Supreme Court in *Brown* v. *Board of Education*, in which the Court ruled school segregation unconstitutional. When President Lyndon Johnson appointed Marshall to the court in 1967, he noted that Marshall "had already earned his place in history."

Thurgood Marshall supports an "activist" court and distrusts leaving the rights of individuals in the hands of elected officials. This distrust is rooted in a long history of political neglect of blacks and other minorities. In 1977, Marshall wrote, "When elected leaders cower before public pressure, this Court more than ever, must not shrink from its duty to enforce the Constitution for the benefit of the poor and helpless."

Again in 1981, Marshall criticized his colleagues for upholding a congressional decision to exclude women from the military draft. "Congressional enactments in the area of military affairs must, like all other laws, be judged by the standards of the Constitution. For the Constitution is the supreme law of the land and all legislation must conform to its principles."

In contrast to the conservative view that the original intention of the Constitution's framers is the only proper guide for judicial decisions, Marshall espouses that "Courts . . . do not sit or act in a vacuum. Shifting cultural, political and social patterns at times, make past practices appear inconsistent with fundamental principles upon which American society rests. When that occurs, Courts should look to the fact of such change as a source of guidance on evolving principles of equality."

In keeping with this belief, Marshall wrote the Court's opinion upholding the Equal Pay Act, the law requiring companies to give men and women "equal pay for equal work." In another majority opinion written by Marshall, white individuals who suffered job discrimination were given the power to sue under federal law, a power that had already been awarded to blacks.

Not surprisingly, Marshall's performance on the Court has been guided by a dedication to racial equality and the rights of the poor. This concern was most poignant when he expressed dissent in the Court's decision that states should refuse to provide Medicaid for abortion procedures. "The enactments challenged here brutally coerce poor women to bear children whom society will scorn for every day of their lives. . . . I am appalled at the ethical bankruptcy of those who preach a 'right to life' that means, under present social policies, a bare existence in utter misery for many poor women and their children."

On other issues of individual rights, Marshall adopts a broad reading of the Bill of Rights. He finds capital punishment "morally unacceptable" and frequently dissents from decisions which favor more lenient interrogation methods by law enforcement agents, asserting the view that, "Good police work is something far different than catching the criminal at any price."

Overweight and afflicted with a heart condition, Marshall is the least healthy of all the justices. Yet, he is said to be determined to outlast Reagan.

THE MODERATES

John Paul Stevens

Stevens was born into a wealthy Chicago family in 1920. He graduated with honors from the University of Chicago, and then went on to attend Northwestern University, where he graduated first in his class. In 1970, President Richard Nixon appointed Stevens a judge of the United States Court of Appeals for the Seventh Circuit. In this position Stevens attracted the admiration of law experts, who lauded him for his precise and insightful opinions. When President Gerald Ford nominated Stevens for a seat on the Court, legal scholars hailed the choice as one of the finest in recent court history.

On the Supreme Court, he is considered an active questioner during oral argument and possesses the keen ability to break down a complex issue into succinct, down-to-earth language. Evidence of Stevens's skill as a writer can be found in many of his dissents. In the Burger Court he was also considered the least political and most independent of the justices. This openness to judicial questions also makes him the least predictable.

When he joined the Court in 1975, Stevens sided frequently with the moderate Justice Potter Stewart. After Stewart's resignation and O'Connor's arrival, Stevens began a firmer alliance with liberals Brennan and Marshall. In recent years, Stevens has voted with Brennan in three out of four cases.

Like Brennan, Stevens is committed to protecting individual rights over the interests of state or federal government. "The Court must be ever mindful of its primary job as the protector of the citizen and not of the warden or the prosecutor. The framers surely feared the latter more than the former," Stevens has said.

In 1983, when the Court ruled against a prisoner who charged that a guard had intentionally destroyed his personal belongings, Stevens wrote a touching dissent reminding his colleagues that "personal letters, snapshots of family members, a souvenir, a deck of cards, a hobby kit, perhaps a diary or training manual for an apprentice in a new trade, or even a Bible—a variety of inexpensive items may enable a prisoner to maintain contact with some part of his past and an eye to the future. Are all of these items subject to unrestrained perusal, confiscation, or mutilation at the hands of a possibly hostile guard?"

In the past six years Stevens has become critical of the Court for its increasingly conservative decisions. When the Court upheld an out-of-date law setting a $10 limit on the amount veterans can pay attorneys for pressing their benefit claims with the government, Stevens (believing the law limited a veteran's choice of a lawyer) dissented bitterly. "If the Government, in the guise of a paternalistic interest in protecting the citizen from his own improvidence can deny him access to independent counsel of his choice, it can change the character of our free society. . . ."

Because he is an unconventional legal thinker, many of Stevens's judicial theories have not won him the endorsement of other justices. Court observers have found him difficult to categorize. He is the only justice appointed within the past fifteen years who does not repeatedly rule against expanding the rights of a person accused of a crime.

In 1974, Stevens underwent open-heart surgery but currently has no reported health problems.

Lewis Powell

Powell, who retired from the Court on June 25, 1987, was considered a justice with conservative instincts who did not let those instincts override his judgments. No justice dissented less. Powell was born in 1907 in Norfolk, Virginia, into a family that owned a furniture business. He completed his undergraduate work at Washington and Lee College in Lexington, Kentucky, graduating with honors. Powell then attended Washington and Lee Law School, graduating first in his class in 1931. After a successful career as a corporate lawyer and admired civic leader, Powell was appointed to the Court in 1971.

He remained on the majority side of most Supreme Court decisions. Generally allied with Burger, Rehnquist, and O'Connor, Powell strayed from his conservative line just enough to give himself the reputation as the most moderate of the Court's conservative members.

Powell's ardent belief in judicial restraint did not dominate his concern for individual rights. In the 1985 school prayer ruling, *Wallace* v. *Jaffree*, Powell voted with the Court's more liberal members to strike down Alabama's "moment of silence" statute. When the Court ruled in 1982 that states could not deny free public education to children of illegal aliens, Powell, in a concurring opinion, stated, "Congress, vested by the Constitution with responsibility of protecting our borders and legislating with respect to aliens, has not provided effective leadership in dealing with this problem. It is therefore certain that illegal aliens will continue to enter the United States. . . . I agree with the Court that their children should not be left on the streets uneducated."

Abortion Rights: It was Powell who, as majority spokesman in *City of Akron* v. *Akron Center for Reproductive Health*, reaffirmed the landmark abortion ruling, *Roe* v. *Wade*. The carefully worded opinion reflected more a commitment to upholding precedent than to upholding the substance of the *Roe* decision. Here he wrote,

> "These cases come to us a decade after we held in *Roe* v. *Wade* . . . that the right of privacy, grounded in the concept of personal liberty guaranteed by the Constitution, encompasses a woman's right to decide whether to terminate her pregnancy. . . . Arguments continue to be made . . . that we erred in interpreting the Constitution. Nonetheless, the doctrine of *stare decisis* while perhaps never entirely persuasive in a constitutional question, is a doctrine that demands respect in a society governed by the rule of law. We respect it today, and reaffirm *Roe* v. *Wade*."

Powell also cast the deciding vote in cases involving affirmative action. In *Regents of the University of California* v. *Bakke*, his vote proved critical in ruling that quotas based solely on race violated constitutional law. Powell cast the deciding vote making racial quotas illegal. He wrote, "Preferring members of any one ethnic group for no other reason than race or ethnic origin is discrimination for its own sake. This the Constitution forbids."

The justice's vote again broke the balance in striking down programs that provided publicly funded aid to parochial schools in New York and Michigan. In joining the liberal members of the Court, Powell wrote, "There . . . is a small chance that these programs would result in significant religious or denominational control over our democratic process. . . . Nonetheless, there remains a considerable risk of continuing political strife over the propriety of direct aid to religious schools and the proper allocation of limited government resources."

Though Powell gained a reputation as the balancer and compromiser on the Court, critics pointed out that the timing of his decision to retire automatically tipped the judicial scales in favor of the Reagan administration. "Powell's most critical vote came with his decision to resign," says constitutional scholar Ronald K.L. Collins. "By doing so, he sided with the conservatives."

Harry Blackmun

A Nixon appointee, Blackmun has shown more than any other justice a willingness to change. Born in Nashville, Illinois, in 1908, he grew up in St. Paul, Minnesota, where Warren Burger was one of his childhood friends. He attended Harvard College for undergraduate study and Harvard Law School, compiling an average academic record.

In 1959, President Dwight Eisenhower appointed Blackmun a judge on the Eighth Circuit Court of Appeals. There, he established a reputation as a careful judge with conservative views on the rights of the accused. In 1970, President Richard Nixon appointed Blackmun to the Supreme Court.

In his first few terms, Blackmun consistently joined with Chief Justice Burger in criticizing the judicial activism of the Warren Court. For this, critics labeled the two justices the "Minnesota Twins," a disparaging reference to the state's baseball team. But in 1973, Blackmun demonstrated a new independence and willingness to expand legal concepts to meet social concerns. By writing the majority opinion in *Roe* v. *Wade*, he helped to fortify a constitutional right to privacy.

Blackmun calls *Roe* the opinion that changed his life; it also signaled the beginning of a new direction in his judicial career. Blackmun broke with the Court's conservative members—Burger, Rehnquist, and Powell—and by the late 1970s was voting with the liberal justice Brennan as often as he voted with Burger. By 1983, he was voting with Marshall in nearly three out of four cases.

Blackmun, however, has loosened his alliance with the liberals in issues dealing with affirmative action, sex discrimination, and criminal law, preferring instead to leave those questions up to other branches of government. When the Court ruled existing state capital punishment laws unconstitutional, Blackmun dissented. He wrote, "Cases such as these provide for me an excruciating agony of the spirit. I yield to no one in the depths of my distaste . . . and indeed, abhorrence for the death penalty.

"Were I a legislator, I would vote against the death penalty. . . . There on the legislative branch . . . and secondarily, on the executive branch is where the authority for this kind of action lies. The authority should not be taken over by the judiciary. . . . We should not allow our personal preferences to guide our judicial decisions."

Blackmun shifted his viewpoint on the role of the courts in 1982 when he wrote the majority opinion striking down a Washington state antibusing initiative. "When the states' allocation of power places unusual burdens on the ability of racial groups to enact legislation specifically designed to overcome the special condition of prejudice, the government action seriously curtails the operation of those political processes ordinarily to be relied upon to protect minorities." Blackmun went on to say that when the state fails to provide protection, the judiciary must assume its "special role safeguarding the interest of those minority groups."

Blackmun has helped to create new rulings that expand

protection of the First Amendment's commercial speech guarantee. In 1975, for example, he wrote an opinion that a newspaper editor could not be prosecuted for running advertisements about abortion services in another state.

The following year, Blackmun spoke for the Court when it struck down a state law forbidding the advertisement of drug prices. He stressed that in a free enterprise economy "the free flow of commercial information is indispensable."

At age seventy-nine, Blackmun appears in good health despite a 1977 operation for cancer. He has said he will not resign if his prospective successor is likely to overturn the abortion ruling.

Byron R. White

Born in 1918, White grew up in the small community of Wellington, Colorado. As a child he worked in the sugar-beet fields and on railroad crews. After winning an academic scholarship, White attended the University of Colorado, graduating first in his class. He also played football, winning all-American honors as a tailback. White went on to play pro football with the Pittsburgh Steelers and Detroit Lions, and in 1938 led the National Football League in rushing.

After graduating with honors from Yale Law School in 1946, White joined a private practice and remained there until 1960, when he became an organizer for John Kennedy's successful presidential campaign. He next served in the U.S. Justice Department before Kennedy appointed him to the Supreme Court in 1962.

As a Supreme Court justice, White has been characterized as a champion of certain judicial themes. First, he interprets strictly the rights of persons accused of a crime. He wrote the opinion to the case approving the "good faith exception" to the exclusionary rule on evidence submitted at a trial.

In his opinion, White explained that in some exceptions, where police conduct was in the bounds of a reasonable search and seizure, evidence discovered but not specifically covered under the warrant can be used by judges to decide a case. He concluded by cautioning that "The good faith exception is not intended to signal our unwillingness strictly to enforce the requirements of the Fourth Amendment."

Yet there are limits to how far White will go to approve the acts of law enforcement officials. In a 1985 case, White wrote the majority opinion striking down a Tennessee law authorizing police to shoot down a fleeing suspect. Expressing his indignation over such an act of unrestrained power, White wrote, "A police officer may not seize an unarmed, non-dangerous suspect by shooting him dead."

A second of White's judicial themes is a narrow reading of the First Amendment guarantees of freedom of speech and press. In recent rulings overturning states' decisions allowing for some form of prayer and for aid to parochial schools, White has dissented, urging the Court to reconsider its former rulings and adopt measures that would allow states more power to decide these issues.

In the area of affirmative action, White subscribes to the view that before receiving special treatment, individual members of minority groups must first prove they have been victims of discrimination. It is not enough to belong to a group that has suffered discrimination, says White. "Each individual must prove that the discriminatory practice had an impact on him." In other areas of civil rights, however, White is considered one of the most activist justices on today's Court. He repeatedly favors defendants in cases involving racial discrimination, voting rights, and equal educational opportunities.

In the early 1970s White consistently voted with Burger, Rehnquist, Powell, and Blackmun, and later with O'Connor. His current voting record indicates that he has agreed with each of those five 80 percent of the time. Supreme Court journalist Elder Witt has labeled White the Court's "mystery man." A penetrating questioner during oral argument, the justice rarely lets it be known how he will vote. At seventy-one, he is reportedly in excellent health.

Today's justices continue to face many of the issues mentioned above. Deciding the ultimate legal fate of such controversies as abortion and affirmative action is a slow and complex process. Our next chapter will review the history and current status of many of these emotion-packed areas.

Issues of Today's Court

6

In 1985, at the end of President Ronald Reagan's fifth year in office, the liberal landmarks of the Warren Court had yet to be overturned. Impatient to make his mark on the federal judiciary, and with only two Supreme Court appointments under his belt, Reagan began a campaign to persuade the American people that the Court had taken too many liberties with the Constitution. Calling for a more conservative kind of justice, Reagan enlisted Attorney General Edwin Meese, an outspoken opponent of judicial activism, to carry out the administration's message.

In July 1985, Meese urged that federal judges "adopt a *literal* view of the Constitution," one reflecting the views of those who drafted it, not the views of judges interpreting it today. Meese assailed Supreme Court rulings under both Chief Justice Burger and his predecessor, Earl Warren, saying they had drifted from the "original intentions" of those who wrote the United States Constitution two hundred years ago.

In two speeches delivered to the American Bar Association, Meese criticized a number of decisions made within the previous thirty years, particularly those barring prayer in public school and others upholding the rights of criminal suspects. He referred to those decisions as "more policy choices than articulations of constitutional principle. The voting blocs, the arguments, all reveal a greater allegiance to what the Court thinks constitutes sound public policy than . . . what the Constitution—its text and intention—may demand."

Critics of the administration's argument against an activist court, say that Meese's efforts are actually disguised attempts to clamp down on the rights of individuals. The administration, they argue, wants to reopen issues that were long ago settled, such as whether the Constitution gives women the right to abortion, or requires that criminal suspects be informed of their rights before police questioning.

In an October 1985 *New York Times* article, Herman Schwartz, professor of law at American University, called Meese's campaign "a very clear effort to weaken protections for individuals." Schwartz subsequently found two powerful allies: Associate Justices William Brennan and John Paul Stevens. In a speech at Georgetown University, Brennan defended the high court, calling Meese's campaign "little more than arrogance cloaked as humility."

As the iron fist of the Court's liberal bloc, Brennan said it was "arrogant to pretend that from our vantage we can gauge accurately the intent of the framers [with regard] to specific contemporary questions. All too often, sources of potential enlightenment, such as records of the ratification debates, provide sparse or ambiguous evidence of the original intention."

Responding to Meese's charge that recent rulings by the Court have interfered in policy matters that conservatives say should be left to elected officials, Brennan said, "We current justices read the Constitution the only way we can: As twentieth century Americans. . . . The ultimate question should be, what do the words of the text mean in our time? For the genius of the Constitution rests not in any static meaning it may have had in a world dead and gone, but in its adaptability of the great principles to cope with current problems and needs."

Ten days later, Justice Stevens joined the debate on Brennan's side. Speaking at a meeting of the Federal Bar Association in Chicago, he focused his criticism on Meese's view that the Bill of Rights—the first ten amendments to the Constitution—should not apply to the states but only to the federal government. Such an argument, Stevens said, "was somewhat incomplete" since it overlooked the development of law over the past two hundred years. Moreover, he said, "the attorney general fails to mention that no justice who has sat on the Court during the past sixty years has questioned the proposition."

The debate over judicial restraint or activism and over the Constitution's "original intention" will likely intensify with any additional Supreme Court appointments President Reagan may make. The argument is also likely to recur as today's Court, under Chief Justice Rehnquist, considers cases involving state and federal power, abortion, affirmative action, church and state, and criminal law matters. In light of this, a discussion follows of the status of these major issues, along with how these issues might fare within the next several years.

STATE AND
FEDERAL POWER

Supreme Court decisions are almost always affected by the balance of power between state and federal government. When the Court requires local police to adopt specific arrest procedures, permits state agencies to follow affirmative action plans, strikes down laws regulating abortions, or outlaws the practice of prayer in public schools, it alters this balance. Americans are affected much more directly by the action of their state and local governments than by the federal government.

Typically, liberal members of the Court support a strong federal government. They recall how state governments abused the rights of citizens by condoning racial discrimination and by allowing the mistreatment of criminal suspects through police brutality. For these justices, the federal government serves as the watchdog over state conduct.

Conservative justices, on the other hand, share President Reagan's view. From his days as governor of California, Reagan maintains a strong faith in the ability and honesty of state officials. He believes, as do most conservatives, in giving state and local government more room to exercise their powers without the constraints of federal laws, regulations, or constitutional limits.

As in other volatile issues facing today's Court, the voting balance concerning how far the federal government should extend its powers over state matters remains delicate.

Probably the most important aspect of the federal and state balance issue concerns whether the Bill of Rights should apply to the states. Originally, it was meant to provide protection solely against the intrusion of the federal government. But as stated earlier, several Supreme Court rulings have caused such Bill of Rights guarantees as freedom of speech and religion, fair treatment for criminal suspects, and security against unreasonable searches and seizures to be "incorporated" into state law.

The Reagan administration maintains that these amendments should not be applied to the states. In the words of Edwin Meese, "Nowhere has the principle of federalism been dealt so political a blow as by the theory of incorporation." If President Reagan has the opportunity to replace one of the five justices who support the theory of incorporation with one who does not, the balance would shift. In the long term, such a change may place at risk many of the rights Americans take for granted as security against government intrusion.

ABORTION RIGHTS

Probably the most tumultuous legal issue of the 1980s centers on the abortion controversy. No other issue has pierced so deeply into the hearts of the American people. In 1973, the Court's decision in *Roe* v. *Wade* made abortion legal. Grounding the decision in a right to privacy found implicitly in the Constitution, Justice Blackmun wrote, "This right of privacy, whether it be founded in the 14th Amendment's concept of personal liberty and restrictions upon state action, as we feel it is, is broad enough to encompass a woman's decision whether or not to terminate her pregnancy."

Roe stands as one of the main targets of the current administration's argument calling for a strict reading of the Constitution. Solicitor General Charles Fried in July 1985 told the Justices that they should overrule *Roe* because "there is no explicit textual warrant in the Constitution for the right to abortion."

The Court has reaffirmed *Roe* in two major decisions. In the 1983 case, *City of Akron* v. *Akron Center for Reproductive Health*, the Court declared again that the state cannot restrict the availability of abortion until after the third month of pregnancy. Next, in June 1986, the Court struck down a Pennsylvania law intended to regulate abortions.

Since the *Roe* ruling, the voting margins have narrowed considerably. In 1973, the justices supporting it had a substantial majority with a 7 to 2 vote. In the 1983 *Akron* case, O'Connor's vote expanded the minority, changing the vote to 6 to 3. The minority gained another vote in the recent Pennsylvania case as Burger, previously in the majority, dissented. The right to abortion ruling now stands 5 to 4.

The decision has been weakened by O'Connor's assertion that the *Roe* decision is scientifically flawed (see Chapter Five). With the Reagan administration's insistence that a constitutional right to abortion does not exist joined by O'Connor's scientific factor, the ruling's future looks grave. A Reagan appointment eliminating a majority vote would probably overturn the *Roe* decision.

AFFIRMATIVE ACTION

Affirmative action, using an applicant's race or sex as a plus when hiring a person for a job or accepting a student's

After the Court legalized abortion in 1973,
the Supreme Court building in Washington
became the site of annual demonstrations
by groups opposed to the decision.

application for college, is the number one issue in the civil rights area. Supporters of the idea, such as the American Civil Liberties Union, consider it essential in addressing past employment discrimination against women and minorities.

For more than a decade, government and private employers have used affirmative action policies, sometimes voluntarily and sometimes under court order. The Reagan administration opposes affirmative action, calling it "reverse discrimination" against white males. Through a number of court cases, both sides can claim victories. The results are mixed due to the complexity of the issue and the division of the nine justices over how it should be decided.

The most publicized civil rights case of the 1970s, *University of California Regents* v. *Bakke*, centered on affirmative action. It involved Allen Bakke's rejected application to the University of California's medical school. The thirty-three-year-old Norwegian-American, who had scored in the top 10 percent of the medical admissions exam, blamed his rejection on the university's affirmative action program.

Here the Court ruled it illegal for a state medical school to set aside a certain number of vacancies for blacks and other minorities. But, the Court also held to the constitutionality of admissions policies that consider race a "plus" in considering an applicant's qualifications.

Basically the decision struck a compromise. Bakke was admitted to medical school, and at the same time the Court voted to uphold the idea of affirmative action without strict racial quotas.

More recently in 1986, in *Wygant* v. *Jackson Board of Education*, a group of white schoolteachers charged their school board with violating their constitutional rights to equal protection by its affirmative action policy. The goal of the plan was to keep minority teachers on staff as role models for the high percentage of minority students.

To accomplish this, the board laid off white teachers before minority teachers to maintain a racial balance. Yet many white teachers who had been laid off had worked in the school longer than minority teachers who were not laid off. The white teachers with more seniority believed the policy discriminated against them.

As in previous rulings, the Court approved affirmative action in some limited circumstances, and disapproved it in others, leaving many questions unresolved. In a 5 to 4 vote, the Court agreed with the white teachers, stressing that racially based layoffs have a severe impact on whites. The Court also agreed with the administration's argument that "racial quotas cannot lighten, much less discharge this burden of justification by claiming to favor blacks or other disadvantaged groups and therefore claim to be benign."

Writing for the Court, Justice Powell agreed that the layoff plan violated the rights of several white teachers. Powell added that government might give preference to blacks in hiring—but not layoffs—if the plans are "narrowly tailored to redress past discrimination."

The Court, however, reflected the administration's argument that the Constitution bars governments from using any legal distinctions favoring employment based on color or race at the expense of innocent whites.

Because the Court is so divided on this issue (the *Wygant* case involved five separate opinions), the question of how far a society can go to make up for past discrimination remains uncertain.

THE SEPARATION OF CHURCH AND STATE

The establishment clause contained within the First Amendment is the constitutional basis for controversy over the Court's church and state rulings. It served as the foundation for the Court's 1964 decision in *Engel* v. *Vitale* forbidding prayer in public school classrooms. And in the 1970s, it served as the reasoning behind rulings striking down a variety of state aid programs to public schools.

In 1947, Justice Hugo Black declared that "in the words of Jefferson, the clause against establishment of religion by law was intended to erect a 'wall of separation' between church and state." The Court's rulings strengthening this separation have been criticized as reflecting a judicial hostility toward religion.

In the administration's view, the First Amendment requires that the government act evenhandedly in dealing with religious and nonreligious groups. In the words of Meese, the amendment was meant "to prohibit religious tyranny, not to undermine religion generally."

In the early 1980s, the Court appeared willing to shift from the idea of separation toward a position permitting "accommodation" of the interests of church and state. In 1984, the Court permitted city officials in Pawtucket, Rhode Island, to include a nativity scene in their holiday display. Writing for the Court, Chief Justice Burger said specifically that the Constitution "mandates accommodation" of church and state interests.

The administration hailed the Court's reasoning, and urged it to reinstate that principle by approving Alabama's moment of silence law. The Court instead struck down the state law, stating that it violated the Constitution. These cases demonstrate how closely divided the Court is between those justices who agree with the administration and those who do not. In the Pawtucket case, Burger, White, Powell, Rehnquist, and O'Connor made up the majority, while Brennan, Blackmun, Marshall, and Stevens dissented. Alabama's moment of silence decision, upholding the separation of church and state, received a 6 to 3 vote. Here Powell joined Brennan, Marshall, Blackmun, and Stevens to strike down the law. Reagan appointee O'Connor was the sixth vote, a visible disappointment for the administration.

Conservatives Disagree: On the church and state issue, Rehnquist believes that Thomas Jefferson's statement on the "wall of separation" is misleading and should be abandoned. He argues that James Madison, when writing the Bill of Rights, designed the establishment clause to keep government from instituting a national religion, not to keep government neutral on matters concerning religion.

O'Connor disagrees with Rehnquist, stating that the Court cannot use history as a guide in resolving the matter of school prayer because "free public education was virtually non-existent" when the First Amendment was ratified and therefore "it is unlikely that the persons who drafted the 1st Amendment . . . anticipated the problems of interaction of church and state in public schools."

The disagreement between Rehnquist and O'Connor demonstrates that not all conservatives agree on the proper way to resolve the issue of church and state. These disagreements are certain to bring about continued divisions within the Court on the church and state issue.

CRIMINAL LAW

The major controversy in this area centers on the "exclusionary rule" announced in the 1962 *Mapp* v. *Ohio* decision and in the 1963 *Miranda* v. *Arizona* ruling. In both decisions, the Court prohibited illegally obtained evidence from being admitted in a state court. The rulings, as we have seen, drew sharp criticism from conservative politicians, police, and prosecutors, who said it would make the job of arresting and prosecuting criminals more difficult.

In 1984 the Reagan administration fired an opening shot on the *Miranda* ruling. In an article in *U.S. News and World Report*, Meese bluntly declared, "The Miranda decision was wrong. Its practical effect is to prevent police from talking to the person who knows most about the crime, namely the perpetrator. . . . Miranda only helps guilty defendants. . . . You don't have many suspects who are innocent of a crime." This final comment evoked bitter criticism from liberals, who said it reflected a misunderstanding of the American system of justice, in which a person is presumed innocent until proven guilty.

Even before Meese's comments, the Court had begun to cut back on the exclusionary rule. In 1984, in *United States v. Leon*, the Court ruled that evidence obtained through a legally *defective* search warrant could be admitted at trial so long as the police had "in good faith" believed they possessed a valid warrant. As explained in Chapter Five, this ruling became known as the "good faith exception" to the exclusionary rule.

In a similar decision in 1984, the Court announced a "public safety" exception to the *Miranda* ruling. The case involved a suspect who was arrested by police and asked where his gun was before he was advised of his rights. Here, the majority ruled that certain situations made it necessary to maintain public safety before advising a suspect of his or her rights.

In a ruling in that same term, written by Justice O'Connor, the Court held that even though the police initially failed to read a suspect his rights upon arrest, the suspect's statements made after the police did read his rights could be used as evidence in a trial.

Nearly twenty-five years after their introduction, the *Miranda* and *Mapp* rulings appear headed for the constitutional dustheap. The Court's current trend indicates not only an unwillingness to expand the rulings but also a determination to cut them back.

Even though President Nixon in 1968 expressed an urgency to abolish the underlining principles in *Mapp* and *Miranda*, they have remained law throughout the 1970s and well into Reagan's second term in office. Yet, despite the slow process of change in the Court, the Nixon justices have remained true to their appointer. The recent rulings in criminal law provide proof of how presidents can carry out their policies through judicial appointments. Chapter seven seeks to uncover evidence to provide some answers to the question: Can presidents shape the Court of their dreams?

Presidents and Justices

7

In the heat of the 1984 presidential campaign between Walter Mondale and incumbent Ronald Reagan, Justice William Rehnquist gave a speech entitled "Presidential Appointments to the Supreme Court." It is natural, he said, for a president to seek to shape American law by naming justices "sympathetic to his political or philosophical principles." But, he added, the effort "is apt to be only partially successful." Rehnquist noted that the judicial branch has proved remarkably independent of the other two branches. Yet, he continued, "the institution has been constructed in such a way that the public will, in the person of the President of the United States . . . have something to say about the members of the Court, and thereby indirectly about its decisions."

There is nothing wrong with presidents attempting to staff the Court with justices who share their point of view of the Constitution, provided that they are intellectually and morally qualified, continued Rehnquist. All presidents have considered their appointment power as a way to influence the Court. Naming like-minded justices stands as one way presidents can try to imprint their political values upon government long after they've left office.

Before he left office, President John Adams appointed his Secretary of State, John Marshall, as chief justice. The appointment had more influence upon the course of American history than any one action Adams made during his four years in office. Years later, Adams reflected, "My gift of John Marshall to the people of the United States was the proudest act of my life."

In this century, President Franklin Roosevelt successfully made nine appointments to the Court. Roosevelt took office in 1933 during the worst economic crisis recorded in U.S. history. The nation's banking network was on the verge of collapse, thirteen to sixteen million Americans were out of work, and farmers were threatening to revolt against sheriffs attempting to foreclose on their property.

The courageous and daring Roosevelt wasted no time in pushing through Congress several major reform laws designed to resuscitate the economy. Essential to Roosevelt's national recovery strategy, labeled the "New Deal," were the National Industrial Recovery Act (NIRA) and the Agricultural Adjustment Act (AAA). The NIRA was created to promote cooperation between manufacturers and their employees. By establishing wage, price, and trade controls in various industries, these measures aimed at restoring industry and production and lowering unemployment. The AAA's purpose was to raise agricultural prices by farmers' voluntarily retiring acreage in return for government subsidies.

The two laws, along with other New Deal measures, mapped out a revolutionary concept giving the federal government authority to regulate business and the economy.

As the court cases challenging the new laws reached the Supreme Court, they received a cold reception. Between 1935 and 1936, the Court ruled as unconstitutional seven out of nine New Deal laws. Among the most shocking of those decisions came in 1935 when the Court struck down two major NIRA provisions, declaring that they gave the president too much lawmaking power. The following year, in *United States* v. *Butler* (1936), the Court ruled the AAA an unconstitutional intrusion of federal government authority over state power.

Roosevelt reacted by accusing the Court of trying to destroy attempts to rebuild the economy. "We thought we were solving it," he declared, "and now it has been thrown right straight in our faces. We have been relegated to the horse-and-buggy definition of interstate commerce."

PACKING THE COURT

After a landslide reelection in 1936, Roosevelt stood confident knowing the American people backed his New Deal policies. He quickly set out to override legal obstacles imposed by the Supreme Court. On February 5, 1937, the president proposed to Congress that it consider a radical judicial reorganization scheme. The plan suggested that Congress increase the number of seats on the Supreme Court by opening up one new seat for each justice who declined to retire at age seventy. By 1937, six of the justices were seventy or older. If Congress adopted the "court-packing" plan, Roosevelt could appoint six new justices, bringing the Supreme Court membership up to fifteen.

Never before had a president made such a bold move to shape the Court. Politicians, including staunch New Dealers, displayed shock and disapproval. In the eyes of the American people, tampering with the structure of the Supreme Court, the protectors of their beloved Constitution, was tantamount to an act of betrayal. The president was nevertheless determined.

In addressing the issue in a national radio broadcast, Roosevelt pleaded with the American public to heed his court-packing plan. "When the Congress has sought to stabilize national agriculture, to improve the conditions of labor, to safeguard business against unfair competition, to protect natural resources . . . the Court has been assuming the power . . . to approve or disapprove the public policy written into these laws. . . ." Roosevelt then accused the Court of operating as a "super-legislature" by " . . . reading into the Constitution words and implications which are not there, and which were never intended to be there. We have therefore reached the point where we must take action to save the Constitution from the Court and the Court from itself." Roosevelt's dramatic and heart-rending plea did not persuade the majority of Americans. By popular demand, Congress rejected the radical court-packing plan.

The president had lost, but only momentarily. In the midst of the court-packing battle, a judicial about-face began taking place. Prevailed upon by Chief Justice Charles Evans Hughes, who feared that if Roosevelt got his way with packing the Court other presidents might also, the justices began to approve one New Deal measure after another. In March 1937, the Court ruled in *West Coast Hotel Co.* v. *Parrish* that Washington State could establish minimum wage laws. The decision granted Congress and the states powers the Court had denied them only a year before.

Two weeks later the Court voted in *National Labor Relations Board* v. *Jones & Laughlin Steel Co.* to uphold the Wagner Act, the first law passed by Congress to regulate disputes between business and labor. The Court continued to support the New Deal by upholding unemployment compensation and old-age benefits of the Social Security Act.

Another judicial turnabout took place in the summer of 1937, allowing Roosevelt to "pack the Court" by replacing retiring justices in the usual manner. The retirement of Justice Willis Van Devanter came first, and Roosevelt selected Hugo Black, an Alabama senator and New Deal supporter, to fill the vacancy. By the early 1940s, Roosevelt had named seven more justices: Felix Frankfurter, William O. Douglas, Frank Murphy, Stanley Reed, James Byrnes, Wiley Rutledge, and Robert Jackson. He elevated an eighth, Harlan Fiske Stone, to chief justice.

The Roosevelt appointments marked the beginning of a new era. The Court soon redirected its attention from business and economic matters to questions concerning the rights and freedoms of individuals. Thus the foundation was laid for the Warren Court and its liberal reformation of American society.

NIXON: PRESIDENTS
AND THE LAW

The episode of President Richard Nixon's attempts to shape the Court contains a most ironic and tragic twist. Nixon campaigned against the criminal law policies of the Warren Court by promising to appoint only "strict constructionists" (those in favor of judicial restraint). In his first year in office, Nixon appointed Chief Justice Burger and Associate Justice Blackmun. But before it confirmed Blackmun, the Senate rejected two Nixon nominees.

It first refused to confirm Clement Haynsworth, a southern conservative, for lack of experience and proper qualifications. Nixon's next nominee, G. Harrold Carswell, a southern federal judge, was rejected for compiling a "shallow and mediocre" court record. The Senate also disclosed evidence that Carswell, as a United States attorney, had backed the conversion of a public golf course into a private club so it could continue to exclude blacks. The two rejections forced Nixon to nominate a less extreme conservative. Blackmun provided the compromise and was confirmed almost unanimously.

Nixon went on to appoint Lewis Powell and William Rehnquist, assuring the American people that their votes would turn the Court in a more conservative direction. While waiting for his judicial revolution to occur, Nixon experienced some major setbacks.

The first instance came in 1971 when the Court denied the Nixon administration the authority to halt the *New York Times* and the *Washington Post* from publishing classified Defense Department documents about the Vietnam War. The following year, the Court refused to grant the administration the power to use wiretaps to monitor groups suspected of subversive activities. Nixon appointee Powell wrote the Court's opinion. To add insult to injury, the Court in 1973 established the right to abortion, a practice Nixon firmly opposed. Again a Nixon appointee, this time Blackmun, wrote for the majority. By the time the *Roe* decision had been handed down, the Watergate wiretapping investigation was well under way. Within several months the Senate had begun an inquiry into the possibility of impeaching President Nixon. In July 1974, the Supreme Court began hearing arguments in the case of *United States* v. *Nixon*.

Nixon argued that his executive privilege allowed him to withhold tape-recorded White House conversations even after the Watergate special prosecutor ordered that they be used as evidence in court. The Supreme Court rejected Nixon's argument and unanimously ordered him to surrender the tapes. Three of his four nominees (Rehnquist did not vote) voted against him. In the end, the evidence proved incriminating to Nixon and within weeks he had resigned from office.

Nixon Shapes the Court: Twelve years after Nixon left office his nominees still remain on the Court. Despite the outcome of Nixon's presidency, they have extended the former president's vision of law and order by not extending the rights of criminals and suspects beyond the Warren Court rulings. The recent decisions described in Chapter Six modified the earlier precedents by allowing exceptions to these past rulings. Considering that his first campaign priority was to appoint justices who would cut back on criminal rights, Nixon did succeed in reshaping the Court.

REAGAN'S JUSTICES

On July 7, 1981, President Ronald Reagan announced his first Supreme Court nomination, Sandra Day O'Connor.

"So today, I am pleased to announce that upon completion of all necessary checks by the Federal Bureau of Investigation, I will send to the Senate the nomination of Judge Sandra Day O'Connor of the Arizona Court of Appeals for confirmation as an Associate Justice of the Supreme Court of the United States.

"I commend her to you and urge the Senate's swift bipartisan confirmation so that as soon as possible she may take her seat on the Court and her place in history."

The nomination announcement drew immediate criticism from conservatives despite O'Connor's own conservative record. Radical conservative groups like the Moral Majority scorned her support of the Equal Rights Amendment and her votes as a legislator, which they perceived as advocating abortion. Liberals and moderates praised the president's choice. Democratic congressman Morris K. Udall proclaimed, "If we're going to have Reagan appointees to the Court, you couldn't do much better than O'Connor." Even Senator Edward Kennedy, leader of the Democratic Party's liberal wing, lauded the nomination as a major step for women's rights.

Senate Confirmation Hearings: Reagan formally sent the Senate the nomination on August 19, 1981. The Senate Judiciary Committee held three days of hearings. In his opening remarks, Senator Joseph Biden, Jr., the Committee's ranking Democratic member, said the purpose of the hearings was to find out if O'Connor possessed the intellectual competence and moral character to serve as a Supreme Court justice. He added that the Committee would not attempt "to determine whether . . . the nominee agrees with all of us on each and every pressing social or legal issue."

Not all the senators were in unison with Biden's statement of purpose. Republican Jeremiah Denton made it clear that O'Connor's views on abortion would determine his vote. But when he questioned O'Connor on the abortion issue, she told the Committee that there was no way of predicting how she would vote on any issue, be it abortion, affirmative action, or capital punishment. She pointed out that each issue before the Court presents itself in a different light, always with different circumstances to consider.

O'Connor's care in responding to questions concerning major issues demonstrated not only her independence as a jurist, but also an unwillingness to succumb to political pressure. Much to the dismay of Senator Denton, O'Connor remained true to this stance. On the last day he declared, "I don't feel I have made any progress personally in determining where you stand on abortion."

In the end, O'Connor won the approval of the other Committee members. On September 15, the Committee recommended that the Senate confirm the first female nominee. Six days later a unanimous Senate (with Denton's vote included) confirmed her as the 102nd Supreme Court justice.

An Independent Among Conservatives: For the most part, O'Connor's voting record in the past six years has remained closely aligned with the Reagan administration's policy goals. Yet, in a number of recent decisions involving school prayer, affirmative action, and abortion, she has shown more moderate tendencies. Signs that the administration is not pleased with her independent approach to decision-making have surfaced. As a top contender for the post of chief justice after Burger's resignation, O'Connor's independence, say experts, may have knocked her out of the running.

Two More Appointments: President Reagan's long expected chance to truly reshape the Court arrived with the resignation of Chief Justice Burger. The seventy-eight-year-old jurist explained that he wanted to devote full time as organizer of the 1987 Bicentennial Celebration of the Constitution. Still, some Washington critics said it seemed coincidental that the resignation fell right before the fall congressional elections. If Democrats regained control of the Senate, they pointed out, Reagan would have a rougher time getting his nominees confirmed.

Indeed, whether or not a president's party has a Senate majority makes a tremendous difference in the confirmation process. Some 91 percent of the nominees have been confirmed when a president's party controls the Senate, compared with 48 percent when the president faces an opposition

President Reagan's
Supreme Court appointees
as they faced the Senate
in confirmation hearings.
Top, Justice Sandra Day
O'Connor and Chief Justice
William Rehnquist; at left,
Justice Antonin Scalia.

majority. Considering these statistics along with a Republican-controlled Senate and two Reagan nominees highly respected as jurists and scholars, the Senate Judiciary Committee opened confirmation hearings July 29, 1986.

The Senate and Rehnquist: From the start, Democrat and Republican members moved quickly to draw the lines of battle. The grueling questioning of Rehnquist during the confirmation hearings of 1986 indicated that a far-reaching matter occupied the minds of Democratic senators. In scrutinizing the then associate justice, the Democrats set a standard, warning the president that any future candidate will have to undergo a similar study.

The examination of Rehnquist began with Democratic Senator Edward Kennedy assailing the justice for consistently upholding government power over individual and civil rights. Calling Rehnquist's court record "appalling," Kennedy added, "As a member of the Court he has a virtually unblemished record of opposition to individual rights in cases involving minorities, women, children and the poor." Senator Howard Metzenbaum, another Democrat, agreed, suggesting that Rehnquist's views were "so extreme that they were out of the mainstream of American thought."

Republican senator Orin Hatch dismissed the criticism as "ridiculous" and said it was time to end the "character assassination." Republican senator Strom Thurmond agreed, saying of the nominee, "He is widely acknowledged as a formidable scholar and articulate judge. His ability and intellect, his understanding of the Senate, and his performance as a member of the Supreme Court are exemplary." Thurmond, as did other senators, predicted with confidence that the nomination would be confirmed.

In the six weeks that followed, Rehnquist faced considerable scrutiny from senators opposed to the nomination. In one instance, Kennedy accused him of harassing black and Hispanic voters in Phoenix during 1960 elections. To help verify the incident, a former federal prosecutor testified that he indeed saw Rehnquist challenge voters at a polling location. Rehnquist denied the accusation.

The Committee again lashed out at the associate justice after uncovering a deed on one of Rehnquist's homes restricting the house from being sold to "anyone of the Hebrew race." Rehnquist replied that he could not recall the clause when he had originally read the deed.

The Rehnquist testimony received immediate criticism. A *New York Times* editorial, in questioning the justice's credibility, said, "He has frustrated the Senate's inquiry with evasive and unconvincing answers. The Senate's pride and serious task of passing a candidate for Chief Justice ought to make it demand more. This venerated post should not be conferred midst so many nagging doubts."

Also, 110 law professors joined in a statement opposing the Rehnquist confirmation. They suggested that he had acted unethically and had testified untruthfully to a wide range of issues, including those mentioned above. Nevertheless, the majority of the eighteen-member Judiciary Committee concluded that Rehnquist was a man of "unquestioned integrity" and "overwhelmingly qualified to serve as Chief Justice." Former Associate Deputy Attorney General Bruce Fein praised the Committee's conclusions, pointing out that "Every sitting Associate Justice enthusiastically and unreservedly supports the nomination of William H. Rehnquist to be Chief Justice of the United States."

On September 17, 1986, William Rehnquist received Senate confirmation as the nation's fifteenth chief justice. The same day, Antonin Scalia, who passed through the confirmation hearings with hardly a whisper heard, was confirmed as an associate justice of the United States Supreme Court.

A New Senate Majority: Since November 4, 1986, nearly two months after the Senate confirmed William Rehnquist as chief justice and Antonin Scalia as an associate justice, the Democratic Party has controlled the Senate. This has made it difficult for Reagan to receive confirmation for any additional nominees. Also, Reagan is fighting a "lame duck" image, a phrase used to describe the decline of a president's power toward the end of his final term. In the past, when the opposition party has controlled the Senate and the president has made a nomination during the lame duck period, nominations have been defeated eleven out of fifteen times. Given these obstacles, one of Reagan's major challenges will be to successfully usher a Supreme Court nominee through the political thicket of a Senate confirmation hearing.

Lewis Powell's startling resignation guaranteed for Reagan that major challenge. The announcement came just as the Court was issuing the final opinions of its 1986–87 term, its first under the conservative Chief Justice Rehnquist. It was Powell's critical moderate vote, observers pointed out, that had cemented the Court's liberal to moderate coalition. With Powell gone, that alliance has been left in a perilous state.

Immediately following Powell's announcement, Senator Patrick J. Leahy of Vermont, head of a Democratic group that evaluates judicial nominees, noted, "The President said in two elections that he intends to totally redo the Federal Court system. He wanted to change its position on abortion, to make some major curtailments in free speech, to change its approach on criminal matters and the rights of the accused.

"With the remaining lower court judges he has to appoint, and now with the chance to replace the man who has been the pivotal vote in a lot of 5-to-4 decisions, he's probably in a position to carry out the biggest of his campaign promises—to make a major change in the federal court system for the rest of this century."

While Powell's retirement surprised even the President, the administration wasted little time in finding a replacement. On July 1, 1987, President Reagan announced his choice: Robert H. Bork, a United States circuit court judge of the District of Columbia and former United States solicitor general.

The sixty-year-old former Yale law professor had been known to the public chiefly as the acting attorney general who, in 1973, followed President Nixon's order to fire Archibald Cox as the first Watergate special prosecutor. Opponents to the Bork nomination deplored his role in that episode, while supporters said he acted honorably. As observers predicted, Bork's connections with former President Nixon gave Democrats the chance to dredge up the Watergate affair during the Senate confirmation hearings that began September 15, 1987.

THE BATTLE OVER BORK

Even before the hearings started, the pro- and anti-Bork factions clashed in a war of words. Heading up the liberal pack was Delaware Democrat Joseph Biden, chairman of the Senate Judiciary Committee. Speaking at the American Bar Association convention in August, 1987, Biden said that Bork might try to revoke "dozens" of Supreme Court decisions. Said Biden: "Had he been Justice during the past thirty years and had his view prevailed, America would be a fundamentally different place than it is today."

Two conservative groups, the American Conservative Union and the Coalition for America, assailed Biden for his comments, stating that he should not preside over the hearings because he had already announced his opposition to Bork.

Alan Morrison, head of the Public Citizen Litigation Group, an organization founded by consumer advocate Ralph Nader, added more coal to the fire by supporting Biden's claim that Bork's conservatism appears dangerously clear cut. "In decisive cases, you can predict Bork's vote with virtual complete accuracy, simply by identifying the parties in the case."

The Reagan Administration, however, went out of its way to dispel the notion of Bork as an arch conservative. Before the hearings, the White House circulated, to key senators, a briefing book that outlined many of Bork's rulings and proclaimed that his appointment to the Court "will not alter the balance in any way."

Caught between the verbal cross fire was Judge Bork who, despite his scholarly reputation, tried but failed to convince the majority of the fourteen-member Senate Judiciary Committee that he was the right man for the job. Apart from his involvement in Watergate, Bork was assailed by Democrat and Republican senators alike for his narrow stands on issues ranging from privacy rights to desegregation.

Announcing his opposition to Bork, Republican Senator Arlen Specter of Pennsylvania remarked: "I believe there is substantial doubt as to how he would apply fundamental principles of the constitution." Specter's pivotal vote cemented an anti-Bork majority. After voting 9 to 5 against the nomination, the committee sent the recommendation to the full Senate. On October 6, 1987, the Senate rejected the nomination of Robert Bork by a vote of 58 to 42, the biggest margin of defeat for any Supreme Court nominee.

Within weeks, the Reagan administration announced the nomination of United States Court of Appeals Judge Douglas Ginsburg. In contrast to Bork, who had compiled a thirty-five-year record of academic and professional accomplishments, Ginsburg had only been out of law school fourteen years—a fact that aroused sharp criticism.

"Ginsburg is a question mark. Bork was an exclamation point," said James Buchanan, chairman of People for the American Way, a civil liberties group that lobbied against Bork. Indeed, Ginsburg's legal writings were confined mainly to business regulation. His lack of opinions on abortion, civil rights, and other constitutional matters left senators puzzled about how to evaluate the nominee.

Also, in 1986, the American Bar Association gave Ginsburg its lowest qualified rating when considering him for the appeals court post. The reason: lack of experience.

"He's the perfect, invisible candidate," fumed one Democratic aide. "He'll say the rights things in committee and no one will be able to check him on it."

Yet even before the senate hearings got under way, National Public Radio reported that as a Harvard law professor, Ginsburg had smoked marijuana. In addition, questions arose about Ginsburg's participation in a major case regarding cable television. The incident raised eyebrows because, at the same time, he held $140,000 in stock in a cable television company. To spare the administration further embarrassment, Ginsburg quickly withdrew his name as a nominee for the High Court.

SUPREME COURT NOMINEE, ROUND THREE

There was little fanfare to President Reagan's announcement on November 11, 1987, that Judge Anthony M. Kennedy was his latest choice for the Supreme Court. The Federal Appeals Court judge had been runner-up to Ginsburg only two weeks earlier. Born and raised in Sacramento, California, Kennedy was appointed to the Ninth Circuit in 1975. He graduated from Stanford University, spent a year at the London School of Economics, and earned his law degree from Harvard in 1961. Prior to his appointment as a federal judge, Kennedy ran a lucrative family law practice started by his father.

Some judicial observers place him in the same mold as Justice Lewis Powell, whom he would replace. "There is no question he is a conservative judge," commented one of Kennedy's former law clerks. "But he is moderate in the tone of his opinions and the way he reaches decisions." Others like Harvard Law Professor Laurence Tribe agreed calling Kennedy "refreshingly moderate."

The nominee's twelve-year record as an appellate judge, however, indicates he would be hard-line on criminal justice matters. Arizona Supreme Court Justice James Duke Cameron said that Kennedy could play an important role in abolishing the exclusionary rule (see Chapter Four), remarking that the nominee is "moderate to right of center" on crime related issues.

Commenting on how little controversy the Kennedy nomination has generated, Joseph Biden, chairman of the Senate Judiciary Committee, remarked: "Unless something happens that I am not aware of, we will be able to move pretty swiftly" through the confirmation process. The hearings began on December 14, 1987; Judge Kennedy was confirmed in February 1988.

THE END OF THE REAGAN CRUSADE?

Despite two landslide elections, critics contend that President Reagan has failed to translate his political beliefs into reality. Running on a platform that included reversing the direction of the Supreme Court, Reagan was forced, after two attempts, to nominate a moderate, someone less likely to carry out the administration's policies.

"It's amazing to contemplate," said Michael P. McDonald, an official for the conservative Washington Legal Foundation. "We were so close to locking in a conservative majority on the Court into the next century." Now, he added, if a Democratic president wins in 1988, any vacancies on the Court could be filled with liberal judges. For that reason, many Reagan supporters believe that the administration's crusade to mold the direction of the Supreme Court might be over.

THE NEXT PRESIDENT

Experts agree that after 1988, the future of Supreme Court appointments depends on whether a Democrat or Republican gets elected and how determined that president is about shaping the Supreme Court. Harvard Law Professor Laurence Tribe forecasts two different scenarios.

In one, the Rehnquist Court will continue the same trend set by the Burger Court, by securing the Warren Court rulings. After a while, says Tribe, it will start to "reassert" the Warren ideals by handing down many liberal rulings. Tribe forecasts, in a second scenario, that the Rehnquist Court will carry out the conservative counter-revolution, once assumed to be the mission of the Burger Court.

Other experts, such as Professor Yale Kamisar of the University of Michigan Law School, point out that political change and new issues arising as a result make forecasting the Court's direction uncertain. For instance, he says, "We know how Scalia will be only on certain issues. He may surprise a lot of people on issues we haven't even contemplated yet."

The lesson of history demonstrates that until a justice's vote is cast, that vote remains a mystery. Justices reach decisions only after a review of the cases before them, and in light of several other elements, including the impact of past cases, their regard for precedent, and current societal conditions. The views of the president who appointed them serve as only one factor.

As William Rehnquist, leader of today's Court, remarked in his October 1984 speech, "Neither the President nor his appointees can foresee what issues will come before the Court during the tenure of the appointees. Even though they agree as to the proper resolution of current cases, they may well disagree as to future cases involving other questions." This uncertainty of tomorrow's issues along with the concept of checks and balances provided by the Constitution, concluded Rehnquist, ". . . make the Supreme Court independent of the President and Congress."

For Further Reading

Abraham, Henry J. *Justices and Presidents: A Political History of Appointments to the Supreme Court*. New York: Oxford University Press, 1974.

Anderson, Burnett, and Harrell, Mary Ann. *Equal Justice Under the Law: The Supreme Court in American Life*. Washington, D.C.: The Supreme Court Historical Society, 1982.

Armstrong, Scott, and Woodward, Bob. *The Brethren: Inside the Supreme Court*. New York: Simon and Schuster, 1979.

Cullop, Floyd G. *The Constitution of the United States: An Introduction*. New York: New American Library, 1983.

Friendly, Fred W., and Elliot, Martha J. H. *The Constitution: That Delicate Balance*. New York: Random House, 1984.

Hamilton, Alexander; Madison, James; Jay, John. *The Federalist Papers*, with an introduction by Clinton Rossiter. New York: New American Library, 1961. Particularly Hamilton's essays on the federal judiciary (78 through 83).

Tribe, Laurence H. *God Save This Honorable Court*. New York: Random House, 1985.

Witt, Elder. *A Different Justice*. Congressional Quarterly, Inc., 1986.

Index